Abigail –
. Thank you for all
you do. Mostly, thx for
"being" !

Gina Macdonald

MYOB: MIND YOUR OWN BODY
A Body Image Handbook

ADJUST EXPECTATIONS

INNER STRENGTH

AWAKEN

the road to recovery

DARE.DREAM

Mind Your Own Body

A Body Image Handbook

GINA MACDONALD MA, LPC, CEDS

MYOB: Mind Your Own Body
A Body Image Handbook

©2018, Gina Macdonald

Copy Editor: Heidi Downey
Cover Design: Jay Babina Graphics
Cover Illustration/Collage: Jen Batschelet
Illustrations: Gina Macdonald, BFA, MA.
Illustration Editor: Virginia Macdonald BFA.
Book Design: Words by Jen, Branford, CT

ISBN: 978-0-692-18879-8

Printed in the United States

To my clients who have taught me the depth
of their being and to my loving husband
for his continuous support.

xoxo

CONTENTS

**Section One: Twenty Questions
Related to Body Image**

KNOWING WHAT IT IS AND ISN'T

WHAT GOES WRONG WITH BODY IMAGE

Section Two: The Experiential Approach to Healing Negative Body Image

WHAT YOU SEE AND DON'T SEE

PREFACE

The area of body image has been of personal interest to me since the early 1970s when I experienced a pronounced eating disorder. There were no labels for "eating disorder" or "body image disturbance" at that time—or in the years to come. It was a lonely and shameful period for me. Fortunately, I was involved in dance with a teacher who urged me to express myself through movement and to fuel my body. With her encouragement I became inspired to change my career from visual arts to movement therapy. A self-written, two-year grant enabled me to work in hospital settings with another dancer and an accompanying percussionist. My experience solidified a belief in the power of healing through movement. Despite the absence of specialized eating-disorder treatment, a skilled therapist helped me unravel important underlying issues, and my symptoms lessoned as my health improved. I moved on to Lesley College in Cambridge, Massachusetts, where I focused on dance/movement therapy in the expressive arts program. This innovative training prepared me to work with a variety of populations. Simultaneously, I sought out a body-oriented psychotherapist for continued personal growth. After completing my degree, I began working in Connecticut.

Today I specialize in a field that once did not exist. Through working in treatment programs across Connecticut for two decades, I have met hundreds who struggle with negative body image and its related medical conditions. I see how significantly this affects their quality of life and also their family's quality of life. Witnessing their arduous healing process reinforces how crucial it is that body image issues be addressed preventatively and restoratively.

The treatment of body image and eating disorders remains a challenge for all clinicians who seek to unravel the disorders' complexities and improve effective treatments. Despite our varied theoretical backgrounds in addressing this task, we seem to pull together as a family, recognizing that various modalities are beneficial. Some clinicians place an emphasis on treating brain processes by providing medication, cognitive reframing, mindfulness therapies, etc.; others see the body as the place to heal, using somatic strategies such as experiential therapies, sensory and integrated techniques. Collectively, we combine approaches and modalities in the hope of lessening the suffering of those affected. We seek to discover ways to "integrate directive and symptom-focused techniques into long-term psychodynamically informed psychotherapy" (Bunnell, 2011, p. 1).

ACKNOWLEDGMENTS

To each and every one of you for all that you have taught me.

Margo Maine, Ph.D., FAED, CEDS

Robert Weinstein, Ph.D., MBA

Armin Thies, Ph.D.

Susan Kleinman, BC-DTR, NCC, CEDS

Peter Rowen, LMHC, TEP

Erich Schiffmann, Yoga Master

Norma Canner, ADTR

Helaine Scarlett, Ph.D.

Shira Karman, BC-DTR, LMHC

Noble Barker, Artistic Director, New Haven Ballet

Dorothy Jungles, Instructor, Rhode Island Ballet Center

INTRODUCTION

This is a short, fact-filled book loaded with information necessary to the development of a positive and cohesive body image. This book has information for all people: young and old, women and men, girls and boys (transgender and transfluid), mothers, fathers, grandparents, therapists, physicians, nurses, teachers, coaches, trainers, athletes, beauticians, cosmetic surgeons, nurses—even politicians! I hope you will find meaning in my words and will come to understand a couple of misunderstood truths:

TRUTH 1: Your body image is not determined by or based on your physical attributes or physicality.

TRUTH 2: Your body image influences everything you do, and everything you do influences your body image.

Knowing these truths will help you improve your body image by stopping the war between your mind and body and imparting harmony and balance. Good luck on your journey to learn about your body image—a piece of yourself that is intertwined with personality, intellect, and spirituality.

To get the most out of this book, try to keep an open mind as you read.

SECTION ONE
Twenty Questions
Related to Body Image

In this section we will find the answers to
twenty questions pertaining to body image.
These answers provide fact and knowledge
(didactic and experiential) to inform and inspire
you. I recommend that anyone struggling with
an eating disorder or suffering from body image
dissatisfaction seek out a clinician credentialed
through the International Association of Eating
Disorder Professionals (IAEDP). The National
Eating Disorder Association (NEDA) is helpful
in finding experts in your area. (See www.ideap.
com and www.nationaleatingdisorders.org.)

KNOWING WHAT IT IS AND ISN'T

"It's a complex world. Sometimes I feel like a chimpanzee."
— David Hansen (aka: Sport Fisher)/The Young Adults

Question I DO YOU KNOW THAT ONLY HUMANS AND CHIMPANZEES HAVE A BODY IMAGE?

That is correct! Only chimpanzees and human beings have the ability to recognize their own reflection. "Although the chimpanzee has a body image as humans do, it may not be as clear and as segmented" (Lougren, 2005).

Chimps are the closest living relatives to humans, sharing 98 percent of their DNA. Similar to humans, the chimp communicates with sounds, facial expressions, and gestures. "Emotionally and socially, the psychology of chimps is very similar to humans," says primatologist Frans de Waal of Emory University (2017). We see this with their grooming habits—it is common practice for chimps to run their fingers through another's hair, not only as a way to remove insects but also as a means of bonding. "Who you are is very important in chimp society. There are high-ranking chimps in the community where a kiss confirms one's special status" (PBS, 2017). Sound familiar?

We, as humans, have the capacity to recognize our own face, and chimps can do the same. However, humans possess "higher executive skills" that chimps do not possess. This "higher cortical function" helps us judge and discriminate, which enables us to evaluate how we appear to others. How you think you appear to others serves as an aspect of body image called "body concept" (Oxford Dictionary, 1987, p. 487). While this function will aid you regarding presentation in society and the workplace, it may be damaging to those who place a high value on other's approval.

"Don't try to understand it.
Let it try and understand you."

— e.e. cummings

Question 2 DO YOU KNOW THAT YOU CAN SEE YOUR BODY IMAGE WITH YOUR EYES CLOSED?

If you close your eyes and conjure up an image of yourself, you are viewing your body image. Your image is with you 24/7 and will influence every move you make and every impulse you act on. It is a reference point from which you operate, and has always been throughout your life. It may be challenging to stay with this image without judging. It takes practice. Later I provide exercises to assist you in practicing the art of noticing without judging.

One's body image is an internal image or "piece of psychological space where your body and mind come together" (Hutchinson, 1985, p. 48). It is based on how you contextualize and perceive information from your "internal sensations, postural changes, contact with others and objects, emotional experiences and fantasies" (Oxford Dictionary, 1987, p. 486). Even though your thoughts and experiences about your body may not be conscious, these may "tint" the way you see yourself and your body image.

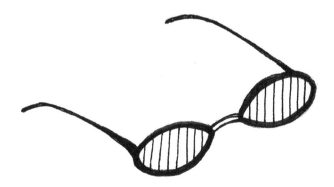

"I get this eerie feeling
So familiar to me now
It finds its way beneath my skin
And it lingers there somehow."
— Hayley Rose Harrington

Question 3 DO YOU KNOW THE DIFFERENCE BETWEEN BODY AND BODY IMAGE?

Your body is physical. Body image, however, is not physical—it's more of a psychological construct. Another person's body is separate from yours, allowing you to see it objectively. This is not true for you, however, as you see yourself subjectively—the way you regard or know yourself based on your bodily experiences, which shape your ideas and beliefs about your body. This is what you come to know as your body image.

Your body image has been developing since your existence in the womb, as one's "body is formed by movement as it is informed through movement." "Your body serves as the first point of reference for perception of space...as a child moves, she/he develops his/her sense of Self" (Canner, 1968). Here we see the child as the center of his or her spatial world, a personal point of reference through which all spatial data are processed. Norma Canner, a dance/movement therapist and my professor, emphasized this important fact: "Body image is derived from internal sensations, postural changes, contact with outside objects, people and emotional experiences." This continues throughout infancy via movement, interactions, and "empathic attunement." "Without this reference point, there can be no relationships—relationships exist as connections between two or more constancies or variables" (1968).

In *Body Image: A Handbook of Theory, Research, and Clinical Practice,* contributing editor David Krueger supports Canner's work, describing the "early psychic experience" as the "sense of self is experienced through sensations from within the body, especially via proprioception." When internal states and a sense of self vs. non-self are discovered, the "outer boundaries of the body become more specific and delineated, and inner and outer are differentiated" (Krueger, 2002, pp. 32, 33).

A cohesive mental representation based on the body's sense of self is a basic necessity for development of body image as the infant grows and gathers more experiences via interactions with others. As one matures, one's body image is challenged to remain cohesive, developing with these changes in social situations. Individuals in isolation do not grow emotionally. They do so through relationships with others. Hence the term "psychosocial" was coined by Erik Erikson to explain the stages of growth and development from infancy into adulthood. Examples of these stages are "trust, autonomy, initiative, industry, identity, intimacy, productivity and acceptance." Any and all comments, gestures, attitudes, and behaviors (such as bullying) toward a person's body size or bodily function will affect them during one or more of these stages. As a result, it is possible to develop body-related "mistrust, shame, guilt, inferiority, isolation, stagnation or despair" (Erikson, 1950, pp. 247–274), as all stages challenge one's bodily connection and the growing sense of reality stemming from a stable and cohesive image of the body as self.

Bullying

Body image is negatively affected during these formative years when bullying occurs. "Being bullied is not just an unpleasant rite of passage through childhood. It's a public health problem that merits attention," says Duane Alexander, M.D., director of the National Institute of Child Health and Human Development (NICHD) (2001).

A study called Project EAT, orchestrated by Diane Neumark-Sztainer and others, researched behavioral, environmental, and personal factors contributing to dietary patterns, chronic diseases, and mood disorders among adolescents. It was followed up by Project EAT II, resending questionnaires to those adolescents transitioning from adolescence to young adulthood. The study confirms that teasing contributes to poor evaluation, an increase in eating disorders, and suicidal thoughts (2004).

Bullying is a common form of abuse in elementary and high schools, and body bullying can contribute to students becoming afraid to eat in public, as they fear being judged for their weight or appearance, culture or religion. Schools enforce anti-bullying and anti-harassment policies to protect their students, and therapists and (if need be) legal officials are called on when a student is the victim of bullying or harassment. Anti-bullying programs help improve peer relations and provide safety for students by offering prevention and intervention training for students, parents, teachers, and paraprofessionals.

One such program operated at Staples High School in Westport, Connecticut. Jackson Yang and Michaela Macdonald worked under the guidance of Elaine Daignault to train teens to lead interactive, experiential lessons to help local third-graders contend with bullies. The pilot project, called Kool to be Kind, was designed to encourage empathy through simple acts of kindness. "Kindness cards" were presented to someone who demonstrated kindness. The cards could be used at a local participating business for a free item or discount. Kool to be Kind then expanded to five elementary schools. "We wanted to start a trend with young children," says Macdonald. It's similar to a pay-it-forward concept, believing that "if you do something nice, it will spread to others and ultimately raise awareness of how single acts of kindness can make a difference in all of our lives" (Daignault et al., 2012).

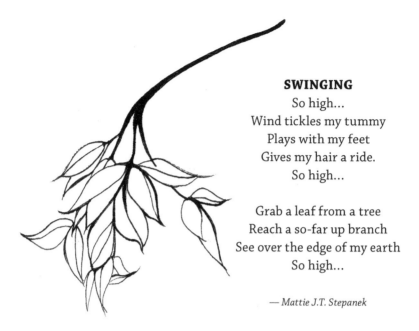

SWINGING
So high...
Wind tickles my tummy
Plays with my feet
Gives my hair a ride.
So high...

Grab a leaf from a tree
Reach a so-far up branch
See over the edge of my earth
So high...

— *Mattie J.T. Stepanek*

Question 4 DO YOU KNOW THAT BODY IMAGE HAS LITTLE TO DO WITH PHYSICAL ATTRIBUTES?

To simply state that body image is a picture we form in our mind's eye—"a mental representation one has of his/her body" (Oxford Dictionary, 1987)—is to neglect the complexities in understanding body image. As mentioned, subjective experience is relied on for perception of one's own body, which differs from objective fact. This subjective experience, based on personal experiences and shaped by others' attitudes toward you, leads to developing an attitude toward yourself. Body image has more to do with this attitude; this inner sense of one's being and the way one regards his or her body will determine body image.

Mattie J. T. Stepanek, a 10-year-old, gifted "poet and peacemaker" who touched millions of people's lives, lived with a rare form of muscular dystrophy. Mattie often spoke of his body, saying, "I am not paralyzed. I can move every part of my body—but I do not have the strength to move against gravity." Despite these challenges, which confined him to a wheelchair, Mattie's body image, body concept, and body esteem are positive, as we see above in his own poetry book, *Journey Through Heartsongs* (2002).

Why is it difficult for people to recognize that physicality does not define body image? One reason for this misunderstanding is the influence of media messages and images depicting toned, able-bodied people as being the only people able to experience positive body image and resultant happiness. This suggests that larger people or those with physical challenges cannot experience happiness or positive body image. This lesson is a hard one for those who assume that an altered appearance or performance-enhancing drugs will ensure positive body image and happiness. Positive body image, positive body concept, body esteem, and happiness are *not* a reward for attaining a particular size or shape. The perfect-looking body is *not* a prerequisite to achieving happiness. The good feelings one develops are acquired through self-affirming messages and experiences. How true are the words of Thomas Cash: "Body image is a profoundly human experience of embodiment" (2004, p. 43).

Working on eating disorder units and in my private practice, I assess many who meet the criteria for eating disorder diagnosis. Many of these individuals (female and male) appear to be "modelesque" in that they are thin, yet they experience pronounced negative body image and speak of their body/self as inadequate and flawed. I also meet many who are not "modelesque" in that they present larger in size. How telling it is to hear from these people with larger body types, who may not meet cultural standards of beauty, as they speak of feeling comfortable in their skin and possessing positive body image. They experience a confident, healthy body image, proving that one can be comfortable at any size. They exemplify a truth that I see over and over again, and which I endorse frequently: Positive body image has little to do with one's physicality, and "the perfect body" does not ensure a positive body image.

Believing that perfection and thinness are rewarded with positive body image is a myth promoted by weight-loss programs and the diet industry. An investment in this belief may bring disappointment following extreme dieting, as one's expectation to feel positive is not guaranteed following weight loss. Mental health issues and a decrease in physical functions are among the consequences endured. I recall an astute individual who joined my body image group in a hospital eating disorder unit. She sat quietly listening to the life situations and negative self-talk of the others. When it was her turn to share, she did so with honesty: "I arrived here today and thought 'OMG, you all look so beautiful and so perfect'…yet hearing you all speak it is hard for me to comprehend how you could hold so much pain underneath your beauty…and I was led to believe you were the fortunate ones." This client had quickly picked up on the incongruence between inner self and outer appearance.

So, just what defines a healthy body image? Dance/movement therapists Cathy Crosky and Lynn Huston write, "An individual with a healthy body image is generally satisfied with his/her body. They may likely experience some dissatisfaction, but it does not interfere with the ability to feel good about oneself, to seek pleasure from the body and to engage in relationships. There is a capacity to be compassionate towards the body and to adapt to bodily changes. The focus is on health and how one feels rather than how one looks. These concerns for outer and inner are balanced" (1994).

There is a need for our culture to recognize the value it places on creating the perfect body and to switch its focus toward cultivating sound and positive body image for its young people. Therapists, teachers, parents, politicians, and caretakers need to model compassion toward oneself, now more than ever, as we live in a culture that is bombarded with images valuing people for their clothing, thinness, and financial success—what Margo Maine refers to as the "manufactured body" (2005, p. 183).

*"From out of the many particulars comes oneness and
out of the oneness comes the many particulars."*
— Heraclitus of Ephesus

Question 5 DO YOU KNOW THAT YOUR BODY IMAGE EXISTS NOT ONLY VISUALLY BUT ON THREE OTHER LEVELS AS WELL?

Body image is a psychological experience based on feelings and attitudes toward your body. It is the "manner in which one has organized these experiences,…a composite that changes according to time, place and situation" (Fisher & Cleveland, 1968). Body image is not a one-level superficial visual experience but a "multi-layered feature of humanness" (Fisher, 1990). This complex construct, originally derived from awareness and experience, exists in what we see, feel, and know as our body image. One or more of these areas may be "off balance."

1. **Visual:** What you see when you look in the mirror, and how you see yourself in your mind. (If this is off, you will actually see yourself distorted.)

2. **Auditory:** What you hear in your head—a "self talk." (If this is off, you may criticize yourself harshly, overthink, compare.)

3. **Tactile and Kinesthetic:** Derived from internal sensations, postural changes, and contact with outside objects and people, it is how you feel in your body; it is a sense of body unity that you experience when you move, make postural changes, or have contact with people and outside objects, etc. (If this is off you may feel uncomfortable being touched, being in close contact to others or overstimulated.)

4. **Emotional:** The impact of all the experiences you have had regarding your body's function and appearance, including the strong influences of our parental, societal, cultural,

and environmental attitudes (such as television and film, billboards, magazine advertisements, social network, food packaging, etc.), as well as any references made toward you, such as name calling, bullying, or "body shaming." *

*A well-known example of negative impacts on body image brings us back to the 2016 campaign for the U.S. presidency when the term "body shaming" became politically charged. The 1996 Miss Universe, Alicia Machado, was publicly referred to as Miss Piggy by (then) owner of the Miss Universe pageants, Donald Trump. Comments were made by him regarding her twenty-pound weight gain, which took place during her reign: "This is someone who really likes to eat," and "It is her job as Miss Universe to remain in peak physical shape" (Maslin, 2016). Machado spoke out against the remarks and the pressure she experienced to lose weight, stating that they contributed to a five-year struggle with anorexia and bulimia nervosa. The story brought body shaming to the foreground, acknowledging it as an issue affecting all people—even those who are "beauty queens."

Throughout our nation women began speaking up. In small-town newspapers and nationally in demonstrations, millions of women and men joined forces. A Branford, Connecticut, columnist, Amy Barry, was disturbed by the so-called locker-room talk. "Words matter, in matters of gender equality and role modeling," she wrote. "We seem to be back in a sexual revolution, but instead of it being championed by women, this time, it is victims, brought to the forefront by high-profile politicians and celebrities who are still living in a fantasy

world where it is OK to objectify women, talk about groping women, and make unwanted sexual advances as long as they deny that anything actually happened" (2016, pp. 3, 10).

A year later, in late 2017, via the social media–inspired awareness movement MeToo, a deluge of cases poured forth. Women began speaking openly of harassment and violations, calling out powerful men who have behaved poorly in the workplace, in the entertainment industry, at Olympic training sites, on university campuses, in government settings, and in gathering places. Women are conducting demonstrations, organizing political events, becoming galvanized through organizations and committees such as Time's Up, a legal defense fund established to help underprivileged women fight cases of sexual misconduct, and #IStandWithPP, an organizing summit to provide support for reproductive, health and educational services reaching over 5 million women through Planned Parenthood.

Throughout the history of the United States, we have expected presidents to shape culture during their time in office, as citizens look to them for leadership and guidance—more so than other political leaders and bureaucrats. Many have failed and escaped without accountability. This shameful misuse of power has worsened, as we now have a president who glorifies sexual misconduct, adding images and words proclaiming body-shaming labels. Donald Trump mocks women, diminishing their value, including Machado ("an eating machine"), television journalist Nancy O'Dell ("I did try and ___ her"), Megyn Kelly ("bimbo"), *New York Times* columnist Gail Collins ("the face of a dog"), Senator Elizabeth Warren ("goofy"), and television journalist Mika Brzezinski ("neurotic Mika"). Regarding a ten-year-old girl, passing on an escalator, Trump commented, for all to hear, "I know, I am going to be dating her in ten years" (Sebastian, 2017).

Such insults and negative comments are fuel for body image dissatisfaction. I witness firsthand how vulnerabilities (sensitivities, genetics, perfectionism) make people more susceptible to personalizing and taking on negative messages, creating a form of self-criticism—scarring their body and self-image.

We need to remind ourselves through the words of educator and activist Howard Zinn: "Human history is a history not only of cruelty, but of compassion, sacrifice, courage and kindness. If we see only the worst, it destroys our capacity to do something. If we remember those times and places...where people have behaved magnificently, this gives us the energy to act" (2002, p. 208).

The National Sexual Assault Telephone Hotline is a safe, confidential service offering a range of free services. For confidential support from a trained staff member, or to find a local health care facility and other local resources, call 800 456 HOPE (4673).

WHAT GOES WRONG WITH BODY IMAGE

"Don't touch me I'm a real live wire."
— David Byrnes/ Talking Heads

Question 6 DO YOU KNOW WHAT
BODY IMAGE DISTURBANCE IS?

Body image disturbance is divided into two categories: dissatisfaction
and distortion (APA, 1987). Dissatisfaction occurs when an individual
experiences strong dislike focusing on specific parts or on one's body
in general. Distortion occurs when an individual believes his or her
body's shape, size, or weight differs from what others see. Perceptual
distortions are accrued and derived from the internalization of a "thin
ideal" body type; a detachment from an inner experience of one's
kinesthetic world; and from one's "body concept," or the "evaluative
representation of one's own body, with special emphasis upon how
they think they appear to others" (Oxford Dictionary, 1987, p. 487).
    Another emotional phenomenon, dysmorphic disorder, "shares
characteristics of an anxiety disorder, and may occur among eating
disorder patients" (Anderson, Lavender, & DeYoung, 2010, pp. 80–81).
We see this in individuals who are never satisfied with their body,
believe they are flawed, and have unrealistic self-perceptions. Time
is spent scrutinizing before the mirror, undergoing plastic surgery,
exercising excessively, all in pursuit of correcting a perceived flaw

related to appearance. Here, anxiety, along with an emphasis on appearance, places one at risk for an eating disorder.

There are immediate effects on both body image and body concept when one constantly focuses on body size or parts of the body via mirror usage, selfies, and so forth. Perception exists in a manner of gestalt, whereby the organized whole should not be perceived as parts, but as a whole. Yes, the human body is made of parts, but the overall body is different from the combination of parts. By focusing on "flawed" body parts one directs the visual field to the foreground and not to the foreground/background together. This can lead to an emphasis on a certain body part, prompting one to perceive it as larger than it actually is. The human body viewed in a mirror as a configuration is a unified whole, not a sum of parts.

It is here that therapists and medical specialists connect the dots to recognize why someone is likely to succumb to an eating disorder when beauty is valued over health, and perfection fiercely pursued. When values are warped out of perspective, one is at risk for mental health problems as well as numerous physical problems. "Body image disturbance is an increasing problem in Western societies and is associated with a number of mental health outcomes including anorexia, bulimia, body dysmorphia and depression" (BBC News, 2005).

Body image disturbance (dissatisfaction and distortion) varies in intensity and differs for each individual. The intolerable and inescapable feelings of hatred, disgust, and shame are known to lead to self-harming behaviors such as eating-disorder symptoms. Diminishment of symptoms and trust in one's body are difficult when body image disturbances exist. "Triggers" which can add more intensity to strong emotions and feelings, are likely to occur if a memory of a personal event is activated by sight, sound, touch, smell, or taste. These personal experiences register through an increase in blood flow, heart rate, and/or bodily tension. Different events or things can trigger people in different ways, and some triggers can leave a person hurt, angry, or upset. However, a common mistake is to attribute triggers to being something "outside us." Although it may be healthy to avoid people or situations that we know as triggers, once we separate from the trigger we realize the source of the emotion is "inside us." This is good news, as it means healing is possible with "inner work."

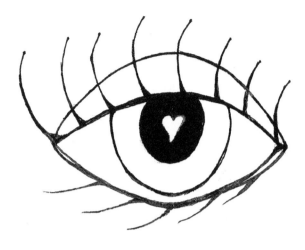

"I stand in awe of my body."

— Henry David Thoreau

Question 7 DO YOU KNOW THAT POSITIVE BODY IMAGE CANNOT BE ACQUIRED BY ALTERING ONE'S BODY?

Your body image is an attitude toward yourself, a way of regarding your body and self. To change body image, you must change your attitude toward yourself. This means to stress the importance of clearing up any contributing factors that underlie a negative body image—that is, self-judging thoughts and behaviors. Paying attention to this inner attitude will lead you to valuing yourself and caring for your body. Note the helpful Experiential Task 13.

There is a societal tendency to attend to outer appearances and ignore our "inner being." The message that positive body image results from changing appearance is false. A positive inner sense of self is necessary to bring value to our outer self and allow us to experience uniqueness with confidence. Your body will give back to you what you give to it. If you ignore your bodily needs, your body will not be there for you when you need it. If you care for your body it will give back to you with appreciation, functioning for you in time of need.

Marcia Germaine Hutchinson reminds us:

> *Through the eyes of love—your love of yourself—acknowledge*
> *and appreciate your body. As you apply a loving gaze to your*
> *reflection in real life, it will become more natural and easier*
> *for you. The more you learn to love and accept yourself, your*
> *body will reflect that love, more and more, and will radiate a*
> *greater beauty that will permeate every aspect of your life.*
> *(1985, p. 123)*

Women and men have every right to change their body into the
body they want. There are many procedures available through surgery
and chemical treatments, diets and weight-loss programs, as well
as exercise programs. All promise physical improvements that will
restore happiness and value to one's life. When clients ask me, "Don't
I have the right to achieve my ideal/desired body size?" I say yes.
"We all have the right and opportunity to define what is ours. This
opportunity comes with the awesome responsibility to do no harm to
your body or your mind."

Beware if you are changing your physical appearance from a place
of inadequacy, as you may be surprised to find a continued sense of
dissatisfaction. Your physical change may not secure a positive body
image, as positive body image is not derived from physicality. The
required work needs to be on the "out of balance" body image.

First, it is important to establish a sense of worth and respect
for yourself, as well as for your body's abilities and limitations. With
that underlying sense of appreciation of self, you will experience
your beauty. How many times do I hear my older clients say (as they
look back on photographs from their younger years), "I looked fine
then, but I thought I was fat." Their negative body image was already
affecting their perceptions and contributing to their ED. It is wise to
check with a therapist or counselor before you decide to alter yourself
drastically or radically. Clarify your body image to be certain how
you respect your body before implementing any plan and expecting
change. Why?

Imagine for a moment this scenario: People with moderate to
severe body image distortion view themselves larger than they
"actually" are. In their mind's eye and mirror, however, they believe

they see themselves without distortion. They wish to decrease "just a few sizes down from where I am now."

Remember, however, their "perceived size" is not their "actual size." If they alter their "perceived size" to reach their "goal/ideal size" the body ends up malnourished, abnormally thin or even emaciated. Despite that weight loss, they will continue to perceive themselves inaccurately and believe they are heavy or overweight. It is risky to avoid seeking a "reality check" which is necessary to clarify your body image before dieting or altering your body. (Note: Experiential Tasks 4 and 5 can help clarify perceptual distortion.)

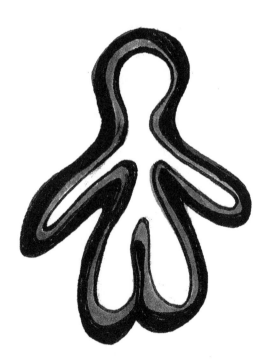

*"You have a paintbrush which can be used to transfer
your insides onto the canvas of your life."*
— Glennon Doyle Melton

Question 8 DO YOU KNOW THAT BODY IMAGE AND SELF-ESTEEM ARE LINKED?

Self-esteem "reflects a person's overall subjective evaluation of his/her own worth....It is a judgment of oneself as well as an attitude toward the self" (Smith & Mackie, 2007). Body image has been defined as "the extent to which your physical self-concept plays a role in your self-esteem" (Roberts, 2004). Here we see how self-esteem overlaps with body image, giving us body esteem.

Unfortunately, one of the few available instruments for measuring body esteem (BES) relies on investigation of characteristics of one's body via a self-evaluative process that objectifies and grades one's body part(s) related to "sexual attractiveness, physical attractiveness and body strength" (Franzoi & Shields, 1984). Hence, any unaddressed underlying emotional and subjective states contributing to poor body image and low self-esteem are not a part of the measurement. This leaves us with the task of understanding one's inner emotional being, which cannot be measured easily.

Body image and self-esteem are mutually dependent in that they rely on each other using self-talk for an inner exchange between the two, and jointly work to find acceptance. Whereas self-esteem can help lift one from a bad body image experience, mutually one's positive body image can help lift one's self esteem. When both are low, it is a challenge for optimistic styles of thinking. Though there are times when it may be wiser to criticize yourself, be on the lookout for a "critic voice," as it may overpower you, leading you to believe such words are your very own. A critic voice using body-bashing and body-shaming words may leave you with dissatisfaction to the degree of body hatred. Just as detrimental is "comparative thinking," whereby you compare yourself to others—looking to find how you come up short. This is a senseless form of self-judgment, and is one of the most common styles of self-sabotaging thinking. Should your self-talk become mean, cruel, and badgering, with weapons such as perfectionism, all or nothing, black/white, catastrophic or comparative thinking, it is time to clearly see it as "stinkin' thinkin'" (twelve-step program slang for distorted thinking). I have observed for decades in hospitals and treatment centers that the body becomes the culprit and bears low self-esteem's bashing. Conversely, those with negative body image will tarnish their self-esteem.

The following letter was written by an adult client to her body. This task was recommended to increase awareness of her body/mind connection. Notice how her critic voice operates—even though her self-esteem was positive.

Dear Body,

I have feelings I would like to share with you. I am sad that at a very young age I was made to feel something was wrong with you. This charted the course of my life. You never had a chance. This is not to say that I wasn't happy. I was always running, playing, bike riding and active. I was hardly ever sick. I was young and innocent. I did not see a mental and physical divide. However, when it was pointed out to me, with a reference to "baby fat" and "not needing a snack," I was stopped cold. I became negatively aware.

I always had a strong personality. I was opinionated and knew what I liked and what I stood for. I was athletic and popular and never stood in anyone's shadow. I was happy and carefree. That is, until it was brought to my attention that you were unacceptable and needed to be changed. I had no clue, and when I turned 12, I was introduced to dieting. I began to separate my mental and physical beings and became conscious of you. Though I never hated you, I began to regard you in a bad light. You were not good enough as my outer shell.

My life went on. I was a good student and had many friends. People were drawn to me. I think because I am empathetic. I know what it feels like to be sad inside. My "not good enough outer shell" became very good at masking my feelings. No one ever knew, and probably would find it unbelievable if they were told.

Now, many years later, I have come to realize that no one's body should not be an indicator of the type of person they are. Not a gauge to measure one's goodness or lack of pride. Our body is our outer shell—it is how we come packaged.

NC

A word about sports, competitive sports, and self-esteem: A few years back, I enjoyed watching a college event in which a female athlete broke the record for pole vaulting at 11 feet, 3¾ inches. Watching this meant a lot to me, as I implemented the first track team in our girls high school during the 1970s. It was awesome to see how far (literally and figuratively) females have come and also to witness fearlessness and confidence in Bridget's eyes as she darted and vaulted full body over the bar with confidence.

However, as an eating disorder and body image specialist, I pondered for days as to why sports and competitive activities are so empowering to some teens and young adults while concurrently common in the development of eating disorders with many others.

The answer becomes clear if we first understand the difference between confidence and self esteem. Whereas self esteem is how we feel about our self (including self worth), confidence pertains more to a belief about how we perform or execute a task. It is possible for confidence and self esteem to be enhanced by developing an ability in a sport. However, if self esteem is low and one is reliant on success, then a loss or poor performance could effect their self esteem. "When athletes self esteem is based only on sports achievement, they feel upset when they don't succeed and it hurts their self esteem." (Cohn,2016)

This holds true for body image as well in that an athlete will react to competition in accordance with the strength of her/his body image. Knowing that body image is linked to self esteem, we can see how it is challenged in sports. Those with an intact body image are not likely to self critique their body. Those with a less cohesive body image might see this as a challenge to overcome. However, those struggling with a poor or negative body image can easily be at risk for body bashing and a resultant eating disorder- as weight is considered "the edge" to compensate for feeling inadequate. "I will be lighter." "I will move faster." "I will score better." are a few of the commonly held myths that foster dieting and restricting. Beneath this myth is the likelihood that strength, endurance and concentration will suffer from improper nutrition—leaving one at risk for developing an eating disorder.

Dance and gymnastics are similarly challenging to self esteem, self worth and positive body image. Perfectionism as a trait has elements of genetics and can also be acquired in (certain) environments that focus on standards of excellence. "Dance breeds perfectionism." (Smith-Theodore, 2015) Ballet, ballroom and other dance types work toward a "flawless" performance as "appearance based" performances. To a point perfectionism may be useful to reach this goal; yet at another point it becomes a saboteur leaving one with doubts and insecurities-placing them at risk for restricting and dieting.

How can one learn to balance self care with the demands of technical training? In the words of professional ballet dance Tiler Peck, "I wish I had known how to take care of my body when I started dancing. Dance is an extremely physical demanding career and it is really important to be good to your body because it is your instrument." (2018).

Are adolescents wise enough to filter through the double messages implied in books and photographs, when advertisements say "find your inner beauty" and the photo implies a perfect body type? Coaches and instructors take note: your awareness of these issues is critical in overseeing performance based, competitive activities and your role is abundantly important.

"In the depth of winter, I finally learned that
within me there lay an invincible summer."
— Albert Camus

Question 9 DO YOU KNOW BODY AND MIND ARE INTERDEPENDENT TO THE DEGREE THAT IGNORING ONE WILL DIMINISH THE OTHER'S ABILITY TO FUNCTION?

In the 1970s Herbert Benson formed the Mind/Body Medical Institute at Harvard Medical School in Boston. His clinic produced doctors who explored the relationship between mind and body. This opened the door to body/mind work and the study of the effect of the mind on health and resistance to disease—called psychoneuroimmunology. Joan Borysenko founded the Mind/Body Health Institute, at which the concept "Sacred Mystery" was developed as a diagram for understanding the unexplainable: environment/genetics/behavior relations. Her theories help us look at disease in a different way—a more spiritual way than ever in the history of medical treatment.

Jon Kabat-Zinn, at UMass Medical School, developed a type of meditation called mindfulness-based stress reduction at his stress-reduction clinic. This technique helps millions cope with pain, suffering, and mental health issues that might otherwise be unbearable. Kenneth Pelletier's focus at Stanford University's Center for Research in Disease Prevention challenged the medical "disease model" by proposing a health paradigm for "emotional equilibrium and "optimal health." He gave people hope for healing through community and connection. I cannot overlook Deepak Chopra, who believes that we hold the memories of every experience we have ever had on a cellular level, nor can I forget the vibrant work of Alexander Lowen, whose "bioenergetics" is a revolutionary approach to healing directly through the body in treating depression. Others, including Marianne Williamson, John Bradshaw, and Stephen Cope, pioneered alternative methods in health and wellness.

The interdependency or "mutual reliance" of mind and body is necessary for our survival. How interesting it is that these theoretical approaches all acknowledge "the breath" and "human contact" as elemental to connecting body and mind, and in healing one from illness and disease. Eastern and Western approaches have finally unified in America's approach to healing.

This mind/body relationship is key in treating health, and many areas of self-care require this body/mind connection, such as sleeping, eating, working and socializing. Taking care of yourself nutritionally strengthens your body/mind connection. The importance of protein, carbohydrates, and fats in the composition of healthy cells, of which tissue is made, is encouraged by nutritionists for an important reason: the food we eat directly affects not only our body but our brain and moods. Protein provides amino acids, which send messages from one brain cell to another, carrying these messages to different parts of the body so that the body part can conduct its task. Protein, carbohydrates, and fats aid us in releasing chemicals in our brain called serotonin and dopamine. Feeling happier can be attributed to these neurons regulating our moods, increasing our energy levels, bringing clarity to our thinking, and supporting better sleep.

Just as food is essential for establishing the mind/body connection, mindfulness is essential in treating the mind/body disconnection. Mindfulness—bringing a caring approach to how we use our mind—is often spoken of as the heart of Buddhist meditation. But we do not have to be Buddhist to practice mindfulness, as mindfulness is about paying attention. "In Asian languages, the word mind and the word heart is the same....Compassion and kindness toward oneself are intrinsically woven into it" (Kabat-Zinn, 1990, p. 12).

Kabat-Zinn talks about bringing mindfulness meditation to medicine. As the founder of mindfulness-based stress reduction (an eight-week course created for medical patients he treated in his Stress Clinic), he states, "Mindfulness is the awareness that arises through paying attention on purpose in the present moment—non-judgmentally. And the non-judgmental part is the kicker, because we've got ideas and opinions about virtually everything."

A deluge of books, workbooks, lectures, DVDs, and YouTube videos on mindfulness in treating mental health issues are flooding our clinics. Mindfulness-based stress reduction (MBSR) is effective in treating body image disturbance for the very reason it works so well in the treatment of numerous mental health issues. The core principles are tools for particular regions to stimulate the executive decision-making functions." Kabat-Zinn and his trainees provide guidance and a workbook to assist you in practicing mindfulness techniques. But body image preoccupation and distracting thoughts can lead you into automatic-pilot mode, and you might find yourself losing the present moment. Here, Kabat-Zinn's "foundations of mindfulness" principle encourages practicing mindful attention to cultivate essential qualities such as suspending judgment, finding patience, and practicing open-mindedness. By "practicing awareness," "redirecting attention," and "expanding attention" one may find relief from the body image disturbance's intrusive negative thoughts, distorted styles of thinking, and obsessive patterns of behavior (1990).

"Change is the end result of true learning."

— Leo Buscaglia

Question 10 DO YOU KNOW THAT
STARVATION DIETS DON'T KEEP WEIGHT OFF?

The diet industry's success relies on people failing in their regime. How? It encourages restricting, and restricting leads to overeating. Overeating leads to punishing yourself by depriving or by exercising with a vengeance, which again leads to overeating. This cycle repeats with a new diet method, which again will fail due to deprivation/ restriction. Symptomatic behaviors such as depriving and restricting confuse the body/mind connection, leading the body into thinking that it is starving, and the body responds by slowing metabolism. The metabolic flame is flickering when it could be roaring. A therapeutic level of food in your bloodstream allows your calories to burn and provide energy. It is actually by eating that you will create a full flame.

The reality show *Biggest Loser* left "bitter disappointment" with contestants who have "regained much if not all of the weight they lost so arduously." A study, conducted by Kevin Hall, of season eight's contestants yielded information as to why weight comes back— despite continued efforts to maintain the lowered weight (Kolata, 2016). The study proves how the human body fights against weight loss. Not surprisingly, one's metabolic rate slows during dieting. Surprisingly, however, it does not recover after dieting and remains slow—even slower, in fact, causing those contestants to eat far less to maintain their weight loss. This "basic biological reality" explains why even the most motivated person will have a body fighting back for years after radical dieting (Kolata, 2016). This also supports "the need for new approaches to weight control" and "shouldn't be interpreted to mean we are doomed to battle our biology or remain fat," says David Ludwig of Boston Children's Hospital's Balance Foundation Obesity Prevention Center (2016).

The sad truth about *The Biggest Loser* is the same sad truth about dieting nationwide. In addition to damaging metabolism, diets do not teach people to maintain their weight loss. Hence, people regain the weight they lost through their strict diet plan. They then come to me believing they have failed—their weight is back and their self-esteem is down. They bring that lowered self-esteem, mood deregulation, social shame, and hopelessness when they arrive. But by working together with a nutritionist, we will teach caring for your body. I believe that body image/body-esteem assessment (presented prior to altering weight) could address underlying self-sabotaging styles of thinking and behaviors. This would also assist in managing both changes and maintenance.

Be very careful not to let the diet and beauty industry affect you negatively. Those businesses are designed to make money on products that people buy when they are vulnerable. We are all vulnerable at times and may grasp onto an immediate remedy. Don't let yourself be tricked into thinking your body has betrayed you or that you are a victim. Remember, you are a one-of-a-kind individual with your own style and beauty. Practice spending time caring for and appreciating your body both inside and out. Yes, inside—take care of your feelings, allow them room to exist and space to evolve. You are the designer and choreographer of your life.

As my clients learn to listen to their bodily cues and to differentiate between them and emotional cues, they gradually begin to regulate both physically and emotionally. It is from this place that one regains self-control, self-esteem, and self-respect. For those with binge eating and emotional eating issues, I focus on the tasks that promote setting boundaries in their personal life and professional life. When people are clear about their personal boundaries, the food behaviors are more likely to be manageable. When you take on too much at work, through an overdeveloped sense of responsibility, or feel unvalued or exhausted, the portions and self-soothing snacking are way out of whack. Should I hear you state, "I will really have to be stricter with myself when I eat," I ask you to halt so that we can focus on your emotional and physical boundary setting with others and demands. This teaches you to learn healthy boundaries (when to stop/when to go)—rather than place more expectation on yourself. Being aware of your vulnerable times and keeping an eye on how you set boundaries is always a smart way to manage weight.

Parents and spouses frequently ask me how they should talk to their loved one about weight issues. Most walk on eggshells, as they fear they will upset their loved one if they mention "weight" as an "issue." This is a sensitive area to address, as it may lead to feuds and tears. It is helpful to have assistance from a nutritionist, who can address weight, scale usage and the sensitivity that surrounds the topic. Registered nutritionists (RD) are skilled at discussing weight numbers or "blind" weights—whereby the client does not know the number on the scale (the RD may speak of the direction of weight gain or loss). How to handle information pertaining to weight is based on what method is best for the client. The RD can act as a middle person and take on the task of monitoring weight, which lowers the parent/ child interpersonal dynamics that could aggravate eating behaviors. When an RD is NOT involved and you are the nutritional support person, it is generally a good rule to avoid such emotionally loaded words as "weight," "diet," or "calories." Substituting with words such as "meals," "nutritional," and "replenishing," which are examples of less loaded words. Obtaining weight information may be necessary for treatment implications. Additional clinical information on the importance of obtaining weight can be found with Anderson, Lavender, and De Young (2010, pp. 72–73).

So just what is a "healthy diet"? Nutritionist Valerie Bryden, R.D., a specialist in eating disorders at Walden Behavioral Care in Guilford, Connecticut, shares her findings: "Simply put, it is eating regular, balanced meals and snacks [based on] satiety cues that our body naturally gives us. Balance usually means eating a variety of starches, proteins fats, fruits, and vegetables throughout the day. 'Healthy' does not mean adhering to food rules that aren't really based in reality

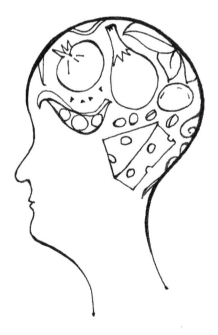

(i.e., never having a piece of white bread, avoiding all added sugar or ice cream because they are 'bad'), and adhering to these rules to the point where following those rules becomes all-encompassing and detrimental to our health clinically."

"Based on the tenet of what normalized eating means, healthy, normal eating means we eat balanced meals most of the time. It means sometimes we eat too much or too little. It means letting our body do what it was created knowing how to do, which is managing our intake through hunger, satiety and sometimes cravings. It also means giving ourselves permission to eat and try not to qualify food as 'good,' 'bad.'"

"Sometimes there is no next time - no time outs,
no second chances." Sometimes it's just now or never."
— Alan Bennet

Question 11 DO YOU KNOW THAT BODY IMAGE ISSUES CONTRIBUTE TO EATING DISORDERS, WHICH HAVE THE HIGHEST MORTALITY RATE OF ANY MENTAL ILLNESS IN OUR COUNTRY?

Body image issues, left unaddressed, will contribute to eating disorders in varying degrees of severity. When we ponder why eating disorders are on the increase and remain the highest cause of fatalities (among mental-health illnesses) in the United States, we are left to question whether the myth of the "perfect body" plays a part in creating this staggering truth. "A distorted body image, and an over evaluation of the importance of weight to self-esteem and identity, are central aspects to clinical ED" (Johnston, 2010).

Eating disorders are among the consequences of a society that places a high value on appearance and thinness. Fueling of negative body image via rampant media messages is a common way that our culture perpetuates such eating disorders. Statistics now show the dangers of social media and its impact on body image, with "90% of young adults ages 18–19 utilizing social media" (Lenhart, Purcell, Smith, & Zickuhr, 2010). Half of any young adult's waking hours may be spent seeking media messages, navigating their world of relationships, and text-messaging to initiate, engage in, and terminate relationships.

Websites, blogs, and Instagram are rife with advertisements promoting exercise and diet regimens, and Facebook serves up access to social connections and opportunities for comparisons. When it comes to messages about body image, the negative aspects of social media far outweigh any positive gains, and provide us valuable lessons. I recently witnessed a powerful moment in which 14-year-old Jenna voluntarily returned her smartphone to her parent's care. This rare behavior resulted after Jenna received a consequence, set in place by her parents for breaking her phone rules, leading to her missing a school dance. Jenna's own words reveal how she weighed the positive and negative gains of texting, making a mature decision for herself: "Too much drama—I don't have time for it."

Teens are especially vulnerable, as body image is crucial to identity formation during psychosocial developmental years. Body image can be potentially affected on many levels of self-evaluation, given the perfection of doctored photography. Comparative dissatisfaction is amplified by the internalization of "social comparisons" when browsing images of others, including celebrities.

Some of the consequences are unforeseen, including potential damage to one's reputation. By simply touching the "send" button you may forward posts and images central to your identity to unknown, and perhaps untrustworthy, people. This is especially dangerous for posts that include obscene language or sexual images. Your "digital footprint" is at that point accessible to every site that exists—and can be traced to you by future employers. The potential abuse of social media to inflict harm via "cyberbullying" also can have devastating consequences. Research indicates that "68% of girls nationally report having a negative experience on social media" (Girl Scout Study, 2011).

School administrators are tackling these problems hand-in-hand with police authorities. Illegal, inappropriate, or sexually explicit postings shared on school social media platforms and Instagram accounts are now investigated as a crime. Parents are included in enforcing protections against ethical and moral wrongdoings as they also might be held responsible for their teen's behaviors.

Students are creating programs to aid other students attacked. In 2014, New Haven Academy students Jordyn Zembrowski, Hannah Sussman, and Janee McMillian created the "Teenage Guide to Being an Upstander," providing ideas to speak up and stand up rather than stand by (#upstandersmovement).

Most frightening are the pro–eating disorder websites ("pro-ana" and "pro-mia," as they are known), which exacerbate eating-disorder pathology. Instagram, Facebook, Pinterest, and Tumblr have ostensibly banned pro–eating-disorder content for years. However, their continued platforms, such as "thinspiration," features content to motivate low body weight, offering other "thin" blogs with tips for starving. These and other sites teach and encourage the tolerance of hunger pain, inviting havoc with the human body as they promote preoccupation with weight and appearance.

The National Eating Disorder Information Center (NEDIC) attempts to keep an account of concerns related to these deceptive measures. Therapists and educators have the arduous responsibility of researching the impact of social media on our culture and mitigating further havoc.

Many women in the media field, numerous actresses and vocalists, are now refusing to conform to the standards set by modeling and advertising agencies. Actress Jennifer Lawrence states how she would never starve herself to get a role in a movie. Demi Lovato sings openly of her struggle with eating disorders. Meghan Trainor demanded that altered photos of herself displayed in a video be revised. These women and others are sending a message of empowerment. They are stepping forward to protect millions of girls and women who are vulnerable and likely to succumb to eating disorders, disordered eating, and obsessive dieting.

"The institutionally sanctioned and economically driven war on bodies continues," says Margo Maine, known for her pioneering treatment for and research on eating disorders. Maine's *Body Wars* (2000) demystifies eating disorders and body image dissatisfaction by identifying the "unrelenting pressures" placed on females. *Body Wars* contains strategies and resources for fighting weight prejudice, dieting consciousness, advertising, body shaming, and other challenges.

Maine's activist guide reminds us that this battle will continue as billion-dollar industries profit from women's products sold with a promise of beauty. While it is not the industry's decision to buy a particular product, it is the "wounded prey in the hungry jungle tactic"—taking advantage of vulnerable women—on which these industries rely to buy their products. Filtering advertisement and product labels is hard to do when one is feeling flawed and unattractive, as we live in a world where beauty and fashion reign (hence the "wounded prey" concept). These vulnerabilities, along with a product's promise of perfection, contribute to women being the perfect target.

Adding to the continuation of "unrelenting pressures," a new image of females presented itself in 2016 when Melania Trump and Ivanka Trump moved into the White House. These professionally trained fashion models became high-ranking U.S. diplomats while representing President Donald Trump. These newsmakers are wealthy women who promote fashion and emphasize beauty. Designer labels determine accomplishment, size is surgically altered, and flaws are microscopically corrected; where finances avail, high standards of beauty will prevail. Modelesque appearance presents as an essential prerequisite for women who seek to be taken seriously. This message to both males and females throughout our country clearly proclaims that powerful women are more about the body you have, the dress you wear, and the money you spend on both. The implication is that only if you do so will you be valued enough to win the approval of the men who run our government. Fortunately, this is not accepted as realistic or genuine by the educated men and women in our nation who believe in values, not in appearance and image. We will filter through the constructed images in search of much-needed mentors, people who are worthy of our respect and admiration yet who are less likely to be photographed.

Our "home sweet home" may also be loaded with body image messages contributing to eating disorders. Lily Myers' powerful words of truth in "Shrinking Women" are resonating with millions of males and females throughout colleges and universities. This is a good sign, as we can see that the cycle of generational hand-me-downs in the family is not accepted.

> ... that's why women in my family have been shrinking for decades. We all learned it from each other, the way each generation taught the next how to knit weaving silence in between the threads...
>
> Nights I hear her creep down to eat plain yogurt in the dark, a fugitive stealing calories to which she does not feel entitled.
>
> Watching the struggle I either mimic or hate her, And I don't want to do either anymore but the burden of this house has followed me across the country.

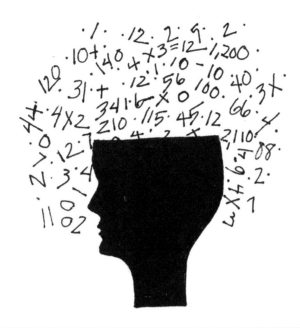

"There is no separation, only in the mind."

— Native American Saying

Question 12 DO YOU KNOW THAT PEOPLE CAN LOSE THEIR "CENTER" AND MIND/BODY CONNECTION?

Everyone has a "center" in his or her body, the place of the inner voice. I think of it as the dwelling place for the self. It is easy to lose this center, as mentioned above. Dieting leads to measuring and calculating and weighing—focusing on numbers (calories, weight, sizes) that are rational by nature. Over-rationalizing puts extreme emphasis on the analytical left side of the brain, leaving out the intuitive, emotional right-brain, involvement. A balanced mind is one that uses both reasoning and emotion—with a respect for the emotions as well as the rational. It is difficult, as we live in a high-tech dependent world...measuring health through calculated numbers, formulas, and external means of inventory. How many times have you weighed yourself, looking for a number to improve your self-esteem? Our tech dependency has advanced at an alarming rate with smart phones and apps, with calculations and formulas for dieting. When you are driven by obsession, numbers will dull your kinesthetic senses, as these externally reliant methods serve as an avoidance behavior of feelings and inner reality. There is an addictive nature to preoccupations and obsessions, which all lead to reacting without awareness or mindfulness in an automatic, robotic manner. It is worth paying attention to your "center" in finding a more mindful response.

Your inner being, core of being, "inner goings on, creative life force, and feeling tone are all names for center" (Schiffmann, 1996, p. 11). Erich Schiffmann's approach through meditation "is probably the easiest way of learning to be centered. Being centered, however, does not require that you be physically motionless. You learn to be centered, and you become increasingly familiar with the energetic feeling-tone of stillness." Schiffmann's Core of Goodness concept presents an opportunity to go within to experience ourselves directly. "Let go of everything you think you know about who you are, suspend every idea you now have about what's true and what isn't, and open your mind to what actually is—so the living truth is you." As Schiffmann reminds us: "For as many moments of the day as you can, come back to center" (1996, pp. 11, 15; see also Experiential Task 10).

Richard C. Schwartz speaks of "parts" that coexist within us. When we get to know these parts and release them from their constraints, our core self emerges through the presence of our centeredness, and they are free to integrate and harmonize—returning to our centered self (2001, pp. 53, 144). Note more on Schwartz "parts" in Question 14.

WHAT HELPS BODY IMAGE

"When the well is dry, we know the worth of water."
— Benjamin Franklin

Question 13 DO YOU KNOW HOW MUCH NUTRITIONISTS CAN HELP WITH BODY/MIND CONNECTION?

Nutritionists must complete graduate and postgraduate training before they qualify to become registered nutritionists (RD). This is a regulated profession, not a certification earned at a gym or through naturopathic studies. Registered nutritionists qualify as eating-disorder specialists through credentialing under guidelines with the International Association of Eating Disorder Professionals (IAEDP). They not only teach the importance of eating a nutritionally sound diet, they also inspire people to enjoy the experience of tasting, sharing, and socializing with food. The RDs and eating disorder therapists work together addressing components of body and mind, recognizing that your relationship with food is connected to aspects of your present life. "If you are restricting food intake, you could be restricting other areas of your life." "If you are having difficulty with bingeing, there may be other areas of your life where you are having problems saying 'No.'" Together eating disorder specialists will help you to differentiate between physical hunger and emotional hunger (Nardozzi, 2009).

This example of dysregulation and poor body/mind connection shows how problems might occur, as many try ignoring their bodily needs in order to change their body.

Week 1
"My stomach is empty."

(What is really going on: My body is trying to tell me something; I deny my need to eat calories.)

Week 2
"I dreamt of a chocolate factory, but I could not get inside."

(What is really going on: I am suppressing hunger to the point where hunger is now a part of my subconscious, expressing itself through my dreams.)

Week 3
"I never noticed that there was a Dunkin' Donuts on East Main Street. Hmm...funny, I never saw it before today. Wow! There is another on West Main too."

(What is really going on: My body is in a physiological state of craving from depriving it food. That craving creates a chaotic style of tangential and obsessive thinking.)

Week 4
"I pretend to eat this so someone does not make me eat it."

(What is really happening: I am acting on a form of denial called "pretending." There is a 95 percent chance I will regain the weight I am losing within two weeks).

Week 5
"Everyone is eating all the time."

(What is really happening: My obsessive thoughts worsen. I notice food everywhere.)

This restriction and deprivation continues, heading to a collision of physical and mental health issues. These include withdrawal and isolation from friends/school, personality changes, muscular mass decreases, lowered metabolism (resulting in fat gain), and the skeletal system's process (osteopenia and osteoporosis—two bone-density conditions). Low heart rate (bradycardia), fatigue, fainting, seizures, hair loss, and electrolyte imbalance are also common with anorexia nervosa and bulimia nervosa. Deprivation of essential nutrients results in mental health issues, such as increased anxiety, excessive worry, hopelessness, depression, mood disorders, denial, and perceptual distortion. The more deprived the body/mind is, the more pronounced a mental health issue becomes. This destructive path is a dangerous one to be on, risking potential long-term damage to our mind/body functions. Not only for you, but for caretakers and clinicians who walk right by your side.

Let's see what happens when he or she follows the recommendations set by the RD:

Week 1

"Peanut butter makes me smarter."

(What is really happening: Fats, proteins [aka: "brain food"], and carbohydrates are building my intact nerve cells and receptor sites.

Week 2

"I ate my healthy meals today, had enough energy to organize my entire closet after work, and I feel alive!"

(What is really happening: Feeding my body gives me more energy to do more—so I am able to be active.)

Week 3

"I accomplished so much toward my deadlines."

(What is really happening: I am focusing with attention to detail. My mind is not being pulled toward cravings as I take in the nutrients.)

Week 4

"I did not get upset at myself today when talking to my boss!"

(What really happened: My mood regulation and food regulation are improving. I am more tolerant of others and calmer—despite stressors—proving nutrition helps!)

Week 5

"My life is running smoothly—no moods, and energy for yoga and errands."

(What really happened: My food, sleep, and mood are regulated.)

"You know life fractures us into little pieces. It harms
us but it's how we glue those fractures back
together that make us stronger."
— Carrie Jones

Question 14 DO YOU KNOW THAT DIFFERENT ASPECTS OF ONESELF CAN COEXIST?

In one of my high school body image groups, a newcomer was listening to another participant speak of her "critic voice," saying, "It has been very cruel lately, and I have had to fight back with my own voice." The newcomer declared, "I always thought it was my voice that was the critic. I did not realize that I could separate from that part, talking back to it with my own voice." Let's look at two approaches toward coexisting aspects. These aspects are subpersonalities and, as Richard C. Schwartz refers to them, "parts" of ourselves that have taken on various roles in order to protect the "self" while maintaining balance and function in one's internal system. These parts' roles and beliefs are taken on through personal experiences as well as familial and cultural legacy. Parts such as an antagonistic "inner critic" may become difficult to live with, causing one to become involved in a never-ending struggle of rejection and avoidance of that part. Schwartz created Internal Family Systems Therapy (IFS). The IFS approach to psychotherapy teaches people how to heal by listening without judgment of their "parts" (feelings or thoughts). It helps one understand that feelings and thoughts are much more than they appear to be and can lead to "wisdom for healing emotionally." Whereas therapists tend to teach clients to "counter" negative thoughts, feelings, or parts, Schwartz seeks to balance the conflicting parts by befriending, so as to have more access to the self (2001, pp. 53, 70, 144).

Yoga master Erich Schiffmann shares in his book *Yoga: The Spirit and Practice of Moving into Stillness* that through the practice of letting go you can "willingly abandon the contradictory evaluations" to "experience yourself directly" as you "come upon the experience of who you are" (1996, p. 7).

These words and this metaphor may be helpful in understanding change: You find an old mirror covered with grime and dust. You begin to polish it. Eventually, after continued searching with an open mind, you recognize yourself. "You must clean the mirror a little in order to get a clearer picture of yourself. Do this with meditation." Schiffmann refers in his teachings to the "misconceptions and those limiting beliefs about who we think we are." He acknowledges the work and the process: "It requires tremendous courage to be willing to release all of our firmly held beliefs and face ourselves directly." And he  validates the reward to come: "One's inner feeling—or inner voice— starts speaking with "more clarity, or rather you'll start hearing it more clearly and awaken to a whole new sense of who you are and how to be—one that contains tremendous fulfillment" (1996, p. 309).

Anaïs Nin, the memoirist and author, was born in the early 1900s, lived in Paris until World War II, then moved to the United States. Her journals provide deeply explorative insights into relationships and her life as a woman. Nin attempted to examine what formed her, believing that we can alter the chemistry of who we are if we have the courage to dissect our elements. She believed that "the knowledge that we are responsible for our actions and attitudes does not need to be discouraging, because it also means that we are free to change" (Nin, 1969).

Nin's passion for life and healing is conveyed in her words and portrayed in this battle between her parts: "How often I tried to kill the ideal self, assassinate the critical self; lose myself...that is—one of them." We hear the "inner critic" and the fight to get rid of the "parts" of her in conflict. Having admired Nin for her courage, I cannot help but wonder what her life would be like if she lived now, in the twenty-first century, with the healers we know today who have approaches that include compassion toward oneself.

"To do is to be."
— Plato Socrates

Question 15 DO YOU KNOW THE DIFFERENCE BETWEEN "DOING" AND "BEING"?

Theorists have been studying the phenomenon of "doing vs. being" for millions of years. Look what they have found:

"To do is to be."
— Jean-Paul Sartre

"To be is to be."
— Friedrich Nietzsche

"To be or not to be?"
— William Shakespeare

"Yabba dabba do!"
— Fred Flintstone/Hoyt Curtin

"Do be a Do-Bee."
— Miss Louise in *Romper Room* Bert & Nancy Claster

"What will be will be."
— Doris Day/Ray Evans

"Being" is the "effortless mindful attention" given to the present in that very moment. It is the absence of thinking and censoring. Simply put, it is noticing without judging. It is in paying attention to your kinesthetic sensations that you are being in the present moment—a form of meditation. Schiffmann refers to "being" as "consciously being conscious." "Being centered and still in the present moment you are presently in." He encourages one to practice "stillness for a few minutes—allowing every form of external energy to stop" (1996, p. 7).

*Practice this deliberately in order to feel your own unique
feeling tone, the feeling-tone of the universe expressing itself
as you. As you relax, you will feel the energy you are made of,
you will begin to feel loved. You'll find yourself feeling this way
inevitably, eventually, as you relax inside and allow yourself
to become increasingly in touch with the loving goodness
that is already you. When you feel the loving goodness inside
yourself—as who or what you really are, you will acquire a
new self—appreciation. You will realize there is no basis for
being self-critical or self-condemnatory. This is a vital stage of
personal maturation and is of utmost social value. (p. 23)*

It may be challenging to focus on
how you feel in a present moment with
awareness of yourself, especially if
you have negated yourself for a long
time. What do you do with all the old
beliefs you hold true? Many techniques
mentioned in this book will be helpful to
learning self-care, and some may not be.
The process of discovering which tools
to use in your recovery is your discovery
alone. One important piece to consider is
your sensitivity to perfectionism, should that exist, as this trait easily
gets in the way of one's exploratory and discovery process. Just as your
critic voice will kick in to negate you, so will perfectionism sabotage.
Regardless of the critic or perfectionist in you, if you choose to
practice and remain present with your simple body-mind awareness,
you will be more likely allow the process to unfold, and you will reap
the benefits of acquired skills. (See also Experiential Task 10.)

"Just say what you want to say…and say it with all your heart."
— Elizabeth Gilbert

Question 16 DO YOU KNOW WHY PHYSICAL AND EMOTIONAL BOUNDARIES ARE SO IMPORTANT?

When I asked high-school-age clients participating in a body image group to define a boundary or boundaries, the answers came quickly and with confidence. "Boundaries are invisible lines and barriers that you set for yourself and other people, in terms of yourself," one declared, while another teen client added, "Boundaries are a limit of what is tolerable—both emotionally and physically." Considering that the group members and I agreed on these definitions, why did I ask them to explore healthy boundaries? And what does this have to do with a healthy body image?

We set boundaries all the time. We do this from that place called center that I spoke of in Question 12. This place within you tells you how to position yourself in relation to others; how to define what is you and what is not you; how much to do and not to do; how to say yes and how to say no; how much to eat and how much not to eat. Setting healthy boundaries allows you to be protective yet receptive. Often we lose our center and react to others—rather than respond from our center in establishing boundaries.

Have you ever experienced unhealthy boundaries? Some signs are:

- Allowing others to define you.
- Giving as much as you can for the sake of giving.
- Believing others will anticipate what your needs are.
- Expecting others to answer your needs.
- Taking as much as you can for the sake of getting.
- Allowing others to direct your life.
- Not noticing when someone crosses your boundaries.
- Falling apart so someone will take care of you.
- Talking on an intimate level on the first encounter.

- Going against personal values or rights to please others.

- Becoming overwhelmed by a person or preoccupied with a person. (MEDA, 1999)

Welcome to the world of unhealthy boundaries. Whereas weak boundaries can lead to not protecting yourself, rigid boundaries can lead to overly protecting yourself. Many unhealthy boundary choices lead to difficulty in relationships, to obsessions, to compulsions, and to addictive behaviors such as eating disorders. When we look at this example (a client's journal entry) we can see that self-disclosure may be healthy at times.

> *The energy I pour into hiding adds to the stress of my relationships and dulls awareness of my own inner feelings— thus decreasing my ability to disclose even when appropriate. I must remember, the more I share of myself, the more likely the other person will engage with me. To be open to another means to risk rejection. Self-disclosure means being real. —MG*

Sharing and trusting are hard to do if a "boundary disturbance" is present. Such a disturbance may be experienced as a fear of allowing others get physically close to "see" you (for fear of being judged on your appearance) or if you have a fear of becoming close emotionally (as in trusting or relying on another). This "fear of dependency and a need to maintain separation between the inside and the outside of the self," stems from hurts and disappointments and serves as a defense against further hurt (Young, 1995).

Disclosing on an intimate level during a first encounter is an opposite extreme example of unhealthy boundary setting—whereby one is not protective enough. My clients share of their desire to please another and to seek approval, citing fear of not being accepted. Their uncertainties around boundaries lead them to poor choices that bring painful consequences. We work to explore clients' preferences in setting personal boundaries by determining what influences their decision making. In this way we can help them establish boundaries and teach them to set healthy boundaries in relationships.

Globally, boundaries are more important than ever. Political boundaries define and separate us geographically, yet we live together in the same world, seeking happiness and respect. At this moment in the United States we are examining how to protect ourselves from those who are perceived as harmful. The concept of healthy boundary vs. unhealthy boundary is applicable given the talk of building a wall along the border with Mexico. We are challenged to decide how we set boundaries ethically: Are we all inclusive, open to those from other countries? Do we polarize against letting others in? Is there a middle ground? As with personal boundaries, political and geographical boundaries define who we are and who we want to be. (See also Experiential Task 14 to assist with setting healthy boundaries.)

"It is only with the heart that one can see rightly.
What is essential is invisible to the eye."

— Antoine de Saint-Exupery, The Little Prince

Question 17 DO YOU BELIEVE PERCEPTUAL DISTORTION IS REAL TO THOSE WHO EXPERIENCE IT?

Clients will ask me "Am I crazy?" when they believe their experience of self-perception is true while those around them do not agree. I reassure them. "No, you are not crazy, as this phenomenon is real to you subjectively. However, it is not real to me, as I see you objectively."

When you distort your body size, it does not mean that you are hallucinating or crazy. Your distortion is both cognitively and perceptually based. Perceptual distortions are derived from the internalization of a "thin ideal," a detachment from the inner experience of one's kinesthetic awareness along with a negative body concept (the evaluative representation of one's body). How does this happen?

Throughout my fifteen years working in hospitals and treatment centers, I have collected many hundreds of body image questionnaires, which I provided to each client at admission. Even though clients never discussed the questions or answers prior to completing the form, there came to exist only four common answers to the question "How would you describe yourself as if you were talking to yourself?" It is as if a secret club exists with a specific vocabulary containing "disgusting," "gross," "fat," and "ugly" as prominent terms used to reference its members.

Like any private club, the bylaws hold ideological beliefs and iron-clad rules for the members to abide by. Repeating these negative self-descriptive terms in the "battle of body image" (as I call it) contributes to perceptual distortion. The amount of distortion correlates with the degree of dissatisfaction, self-loathing, and obsession you feel in regard to yourself. Real or imagined "flaws," based on a disconnect from kinesthetic awareness, an unrealistic  ideal body image, and a negative evaluation of your body, are what you see. It is not uncommon for my clients who experience strong dissatisfaction to see as much as four inches of distortion! As compassionate people and therapists, we need to imagine being in their body and ask "What does it feel like?" before we label them crazy.

GUIDANCE: For therapists or caretakers who engage in a debate with clients regarding perceived size, it may be helpful to remember that years of negative feelings accumulated into negative ideas and images have led them to this point. Body image perception is real to them as they rely on their subjective self. "Validation means the acknowledgement of that which is real. It does not mean validating that which is invalid" (Lenehan, 1997, p. 356). Therefore, validation does not mean that we agree with their body image perception. It means that we come to understand—as best we can—what it feels like living in their bodies.

Validating one's dissatisfaction/distortion means listening to and hearing personal experiences so as to acknowledge they are being heard without judgment. Validation, when provided with care, will help lessen reliance on distortion as it sooths and calms a client's distress. However, it is first important to understand that distortion serves as a protection against further hurt, as fear of being fat or being labeled "fat" may very well stem from feeling judged, unloved, lonely, abandoned, or violated. The journey of recovery will involve a struggle with each "absolute certainty" before recognizing that those perceptions are "tinted." Marsha Lenehan, founder of dialectical behavioral therapy, draws on both Zen teachings and more traditional Western practice. Her teachings for therapists include six Levels of Validation: "1. Listening and observing. 2. Accurate reflection. 3. Articulating the unverbalized. 4. Validating in terms of sufficient (but not necessarily valid) causes. 5. Validating as reasonable in the moment. 6. Treating the person as valid-radical genuineness." Linehan emphasizes therapists' need to accept clients just as they are, despite the desire for immediate change. The acceptance strategies are balanced by clients' learning "change" strategies—as in problem-solving skills (1997, pp. 360–391). Validation, used appropriately (as clichéd as it sounds), is our most important tool in working toward strengthening clinical progress.

BELIEVING IN CHANGE

"With your head full of brains and your shoes full of feet,
Your too smart to go down any not so good street."
— Theodor Seuss Geisel aka: Dr. Seuss

Question 18 DO YOU KNOW HOW TO DETERMINE YOUR LEVEL OF DISSATISFACTION?

Thomas Cash and Thomas Pruzinsky state, "There is little question that our ignorance about the influence of body image on quality of life helps perpetuate untold amounts of human suffering" (2004, p. 177). We rely on assessments based on appearance, evaluation and perception of body and bodily functions, compartmentalization of body parts, kinesthetic awareness, body schema, and value of the body. "It is difficult to know how many different dimensions of assessment are needed to assess adequately the full range of potentially important areas of body image concern in any specific patient population" (2004, p. 175).

The assessment serves as an "intake" of one's body focused attitudes, styles of thinking, rituals and myths. It will help determine what contributes and fuels a client's level of dissatisfaction and provide a starting place to begin lessening that dissatisfaction, which as we know contributes to developing maladaptive coping strategies such as eating disorders.

When a client looks at these, they may feel uncomfortable. It is important to have someone trained available to discuss those responses.

GUIDANCE: *Reviewing these questions with a client gives them a chance to see how much of their time is spent checking, measuring, calculating, weighing, and managing body surveillance. I recommend only one issue be addressed—until an improvement is noted. Examples include the use of a scale from three times per day, decreasing to one time per day, decreasing to one time per week and eventually to one time per month. Similarity, practicing "allowing" a compliment, increasing "receiving" positive feedback as one is decreasing the frequency of "rejecting" compliments. While conducting this assessment, it is important to support the client, giving them permission to share (perhaps for the first time) their unspoken truths.*

Body Image Questionnaire

1. Describe your body as if you were speaking to yourself.

2. Do you have negative self-talk related to your body? To food?

3. Do you focus on specific body parts? Which ones?

4. Do you use a mirror frequently?

5. Do you overestimate the size of your body?

6. Do you know hunger and fullness sensations?

7. Do you weigh yourself daily? Weekly?

8. Do you compete with others to lose weight?

9. Do you compare yourself to others?

10. Do you exercise excessively?

11. Do you refrain from social situations where food is present?

12. Do you use social media or magazines to compare yourself to others?

13. Do you ask others how you look?

14. Can you receive a compliment from a friend?

15. Do you experience mood changes related to appearance?

16. Do you seek perfection in appearance or presentation?

17. Do you ever feel shameful about behaviors related to food? To your body?

18. Do you fear being fat?

19. How long have you been dissatisfied with your body?

(Adapted from brochure "Understanding Body Image Problems," Renfrew Center Foundation, 2010)

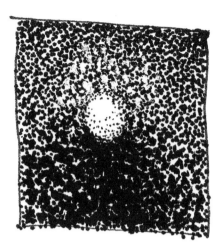

"We do not see things as they are, we see them as we are."

— Angela Anaïs Juana Antolina Rosa Edelmira (aka: Anaïs Nin)

Question 19 DID YOU KNOW THAT
BODY IMAGE DISSATISFACTION IS TREATABLE?

Body image has been a field of interest with the American Dance Therapy Association since its beginning in 1966. The pioneers studied "how the body and mind intersect in health and movement." Because body image begins with movement (as one relates to their environment and others to facilitate change and growth), ADTA research focuses on the positive development of body image, stating "research shows that body image is changeable and treatable" (Crosky & Huston, 1994).

We know someone can be classically beautiful while experiencing a negative body image, while others who may not possess the attributes that our culture would define as attractive, can have a very healthy body image. Knowing these facts may help us to understand more of the complexities when treating body image issues. Body image is not fixed or set. Rather, it changes throughout your life—sometimes from day to day. "This proves you can change your attitudes and modify your perceptions to create a more acceptable and healthier body image" (Crosky & Huston, 1994).

Changing negative body image requires hard work to reach acceptance. Given the many diet programs and techniques available, changing your physical self is much easier than changing your body image, and more likely to be sought out to relieve dissatisfaction. Adding to this is what I call a "ghost image" (an image that lingers despite changes in actual size). Without an accurate sense of your size, it is difficult to know what you are changing.

It is not uncommon to hear teens talk of being "heavy as a child," being bullied and labeled as fat, leaving him or her the predictable consequence of starving to lose weight. They speak of how they radically changed their body size. I often ask, "Did that help you accept your body?" "No," they respond, with a long sigh of disappointment. Why would it? The negative body image issue was never addressed despite altering body size, leaving a "ghost image" in place. This confirms the fact: one's physical self is separate from perception of physical. Sadly, perceptions remain the same; the brain repeats the word "ugly" "louder and more often" and he/she stares into the mirror—fueling the symptoms and continuing the psyche of an eating-disordered adolescent.

Was poor body image placing him/her at risk to begin with? Is the problem that they are labeled "fat"? Is it sensitivity and low self-esteem? Genetics? Gender? Poor nutrition? Trauma in his/her past? How do these biopsychosocial factors add up to her ED? Margo Maine and Douglas Bunnell speak of this as a "perfect biopsychosocial storm" in describing a multilevel concept including gender, culture, and genetic predisposition (2010, pp. 3–4). Changing body image at this point—following repeated episodes of self-beaten esteem, years of subjectively laden information and an unrealistic idealized image (add to the mix a strong dose of self-hatred)—is no simple task for clinicians.

Yet, there is good news here as treatment facilities are opening throughout the United States offering specialized eating disorder care. Most, but not all include a multi-disciplinary treating team approach with nutritional therapy, family-based therapy, and body image therapy. More than ever, programs provide the appropriate level of care to effectively address varied types of eating disorder while educating loved ones. I applaud this new era of enhanced awareness that will expedite effective intervention and provide support for those in need.

"Close your eyes and picture the sun."

— Pomponius Atticus

Question 20 DO YOU KNOW HOW
TO CLARIFY DISTORTED BODY IMAGE?

To change your ideas of yourself you will need to be willing to allow
for the possibility of seeing yourself differently than you actually
are. This means giving up the old ideas and ways of thinking and
"reframing" yourself with positive thoughts. At this point, whatever
you are afraid of (losing control, being right, etc.) is meant to go.
You will be better off with a change in your perception. Resisting
change (the inevitable) doesn't work. There is something waiting to
be discovered with your process of awareness and change. Marcia
Germaine Hutchinson speaks of affirmations as "antidotes to the toxic
messages you feed yourself" (1985, p. 216).

When practicing the affirming statements on page 65 you will
certainly have emotions coming to the surface. Instead of avoiding,
ignoring, or resisting an emotion, practice entering it fully—
allowing the emotion to "just be." Yes, these positive self-thoughts,

statements, and behaviors will not "fit," as they are not familiar in your mind. Once learning to allow positive thoughts to be present, the unexpected—perhaps a full breath, perhaps a new instinct, a new appreciation, or perhaps a serendipitous act will come to you. Be open to it all and see what unknown opportunities may come your way— just by practicing the art of letting go. Through practicing letting go and being open to new possibilities you can see yourself differently and gain clarity.

Ways To Love Your Body Image

1. Think of your body as the vehicle to your dreams. Honor it. Respect it. Fuel it.

2. Become aware of what your body can do each day. Write it. Read it and add to it often.

3. Walk with your head held high, supported by pride and confidence in yourself as a person.

4. Be your body's friend and supporter, not its enemy.

5. Every morning when you wake up, thank your body for resting and rejuvenating itself so you can enjoy the day.

6. Every evening when you go to bed, tell your body how much you appreciate what it has allowed you to do throughout the day.

7. Find a method of exercise that you enjoy and do it regularly. Do not exercise to lose weight or to fight your body. Do it to make your body healthy and strong and because it makes you feel good.

8. Stick a sign on each mirror saying, "I'm beautiful inside and out."

9. Choose to find the beauty in the world and in yourself.

10. Eat when you are hungry. Rest when you are tired. Surround yourself with people that remind you of inner strength and beauty.

(Borrowed from Maine, 2000, p. 14)

Susan Kleinman, a board-certified dance/movement therapist and certified eating-disorder specialist uses dance/movement therapy in her treatment of eating disorders at the Renfrew Center of Florida. She reminds us of the need to reinhabit the body as a place of knowledge. This approach is very different from teaching a client to read their emotions or describe them—or from assisting one in reframing internalized messages they hold to be true for themselves, as these work from the brain to the body.

The dance/movement therapy approach works from an inner sense to reintegrate that broken body-mind relationship. "Reclaiming the intact self requires that clients transform their shattered self into a state of wholeness and connectedness" (Ressler, Kleinman, & Mott, 2010, p. 406). Such a process requires kinesthetic awareness or "the ability to experience feelings and sensations inwardly—turning to the body first to discover awareness of feelings before thinking "What am I feeling?" (Kleinman & Hall, 2006). In Experiential Task No. 18, I delve into the dance/movement therapy approach as a healing method to assist my clients in reclaiming body and self as one.

Yes, body image is treatable. However, it is not an easy undertaking to reconnect with one's lost body/self to recreate a cohesive mental representation. I commend anyone who carves into their lives a period of time to participate in a treatment program every day for weeks—sometimes months. This work continues through difficult transitions into other phases until the rewards manifest. It takes time to modify these attitudes, perceptions, and behaviors based in your bodily experiences and body image. As in grieving, one is letting go of attachments and memories (painful ones), and although it may not be an obvious loss, it counts as a loss when changing lifelong perceptions, attitudes, and behaviors. Harold Bloomfield's easy-to-read self-help book *How to Survive the Loss of a Love* helps one to see the stages, understand loss, and begin "surviving, healing and growing" as well. His "limbo loss" may be a more accurate description as one is struggling with the questions of "Is it a gain?" or "Is it a loss?" The stages of loss always take time, and that can be difficult to face.

Remember the results from clarifying your body image will surprise you and lead you into a world of change—full of exciting possibilities for growth. It is always rewarding to see hard work come to fruition, bringing people the happiness they so deserve. What can make this journey more tolerable? Group sessions, body image groups, art classes, twelve-step groups, support groups, spiritual groups, cooking groups, walking groups, meditation sessions, music jams, knitting groups, yoga sessions, ballet, Tai Chi and martial arts classes—all in their own unique way connect people. Start something you believe in and you will be surprised how it will flourish. I have been fortunate to teach yoga for twenty years (following training with Erich Schiffmann) in a small community called Stony Creek in Connecticut. How true that yoga means "yoke" or connection, as it was my sister who connected me to Schiffmann's video (*Ali MacGraw: Yoga, Mind, and Body,* 1994), and it was through teaching yoga that I met my husband. Even these days in our yoga sessions, sixteen-year-old Maissi, who attended while in her "yogini mom's" womb, rejoins us. Our commonality comes from sharing the changes together—finding community. Joan Borysenko's words inspire us to engage in a larger whole as we "cultivate balance" in our busy lives. "Unless you leave time to recreate, the inner wellspring will dry up and you will not be able to bring forth your creative gifts" (1988 p. 84).

SECTION TWO
An Experiential Approach
to Healing Negative Body Image

Moving, drawing, painting, sculpting, acting, writing, and singing all help us get out of our head and into an experience—without a preconceived idea. The American artist Jackson Pollock explored the meaning of his life and redefined painting to include dripping, splattering, flinging, and hurling paint from sticks, brushes, and buckets, proving that "technique is just a means of arriving at a statement" (Pollock, 1949). The choreographer and dancer Twyla Tharp broke out of traditional ballet mode in the mid-1960s, combining different forms of movement (including hip-hop) to expand the boundaries of dance, morphing ballet into improvisation. By taking the focus away from the esthetic merits of the work in the creative process, you give yourself permission to remove the critic role and act with less inhibition from your "right brain." You are then free to explore different forms of expression, to discover what resonates with them.

We are all created with inner qualities and valuable traits, and these innate resources are available to us through a creative process. I am a believer in expressive therapies, creative art therapies, and experiential methods to heal and reintegrate the broken spirit, the dismantled body, and the loss of one's creative self. Utilizing expressive/creative art therapies makes sense to me, as clients tend to be consumed by rational thoughts that distance them from the body and its emotional self. "Research in experiential approaches supports the utilization of these methods, which often result in a synergy that provides a powerful means for treating body image disturbance" (Cash, 2012).

Experiential learning approaches (movement, art, poetry, and role-play techniques, for example) challenge clients to explore their human behavior in a new way. Through these creative/expressive art therapies we offer "an environment to develop a symbolic language which can provide access to acknowledged feelings and a means of integrating them" (Dokter, 1995). Here, we focus as therapists not on the "aesthetic merits of their work, but on the therapeutic process." This approach is psychodynamic and symptom based in that body image disturbance presents strong dissatisfaction and distortion. One's unconscious thoughts and emotions related to their symptoms can be more easily expressed and explored in the sessions. "What we call their symptoms, they call their salvation" (Boris, 1984). As therapists, we approach and proceed gently, honoring abilities and limitations equally, recognizing how reliant one's "maladaptive behaviors" are to their functioning.

Dance/movement therapists are among the creative art therapists who explore a modality (movement) for its therapeutic value in the development of body image. D/MTs are trained to practice the emerging field of body image therapy, which addresses how you see yourself (perception), how you feel in your body (kinesthetic and proprioceptive senses), and how you think you appear to others (body concept). Working from "inner" (referring to how it feels to be living in your body) is direct and effective in treating body image issues. Working from "outer" (as in talking about or referring to your body) may assist you in reframing attitudes and beliefs that influence body image; however, a common trap for therapist and client is engaging in discussions that focus on body parts such as "stomach or abs"— objectifying rather than exploring the emotional truth underneath. In recognizing the body as a place that holds truth, we remind clients to invite their body into the session and consider their body a friend rather than a foe. The following experiential exercises are provided for creative arts therapists (NCCATA), art therapists (AATA), dance/ movement therapists (ADTA), drama therapists (RDA), and certified yoga instructors (YTT). Licensure in the specific field of expressive/ creative art therapies, as well as eating-disorder certification through the International Association of Eating Disorder Professionals (IAEDP), is recommended. For more info on the required training in these fields, refer to websites listed in the References.

WHAT YOU SEE AND DON'T SEE

Experiential Task I UNDERSTANDING PERCEPTION

Perception is the ability to become aware of something through your senses. In this case, you are exploring by using your visual senses as you take in your environment. You analyze and give meaning to what you see. Here it is possible to create a "visual illusion" whereby you see the object getting larger the longer you focus on it. It begins to look smaller if you shift and look at it in relation to the object(s) next to it. "Perceptual illusions occur when the stimulus contains misleading cues that give rise to inaccurate or impossible perceptions" (Psychology 101 Online).

> **PROP:** A small object such as an orange or a vase that is placed on a table

> **TASK: For a full two minutes, focus on the object and carefully notice its...**

A. shape
B. color
C. texture

D. shadows
E. angles
F. curves

1. Look away from the object to include the surface it is placed on for 10 seconds

2. Return to viewing the object

3. Ask "What changes, if any, do I see in the object?"

4. Discuss perception. Ask, "What does this task suggest? What have you learned from this task?"

5. Allow the discussion to continue as members relate this to "mirror usage" compartmentalizing, and distortion of their body.

Experiential Task 2 CHECKING ONE'S OWN PERCEPTION

Clients will experience body perceptual distortion in varying degrees as evidenced by overestimation of their size and shape.

Body image assessment techniques vary in their approach, with some addressing attitudes developed toward one's body and some addressing one's perceptions and misperceptions, as in this task. "Understanding the dynamic interplay of a person's variables (e.g., body image traits, physical characteristics, and personality attributes) and contextual events is crucial to our appreciation of body image fluidity in everyday life" (Cash, 2004, p. 163).

This useful perceptual task has evolved over years in my practice and is for those clients who want to determine if their perception is distorted. The assessment tool is far from sophisticated, however, I have found it to be helpful as it correlates with results from the clients BI assessment (Question 18). Therefore, I sometimes do this task following the questionnaire to see how one's level of dissatisfaction correlates with the amount of distortion (mild, moderate, severe).

PROP: Ten feet of open space in front of you

PREP: Stand near the individual but allow ten feet of space.

TASK: Instruct the individual, "If comfortable...

1. "Close your eyes. Find a solid, grounded place, connecting below to the earth as well as the sky above." "With this alignment, connect to your breath and...

2. "Imagine seeing yourself in a full-length mirror. Let me know when you do."

3. "Keeping your eyes closed, reach out your arms and hands and place them on your imaginary waist as you see it in the mirror."

4. "Keep your body still as you open your eyes."

> GUIDANCE: At this point, the therapist stands in front of the individual.

5. Say, "I am going to guide your arms straight back to make certain the arms or hands do not turn inward or outward as they move back. Straight back, like railroad tracks."

6. Guide the individual to look down and "notice any space between hands and waist"—making sure their hands stop at their waist. "The distance between their hand and waist determines the degree of distortion present."

7. Discuss with individual: "What do you see?"

8. Discuss with individual: "What does this mean to you? What does this tell you? How does this difference affect your eating habits? Social life?" Invite the group observers (if there are any) to join in the discussion and ask them to share their thoughts.

Experiential Task 3 THE MIRROR PERCEPTION TASK

For those use a mirror more than five minutes per day, focusing on specific sections of your body, this task will help you see yourself more accurately.

PROP: A full-length mirror placed against the wall (do not tilt or prop the mirror)

> GUIDANCE: Group members sit on the sides of room to witness and observe.

TASK: Instruct your client to do the following.

1. Walk up to a full-length mirror and stop where you feel comfortable.

2. View yourself in the mirror—just as you normally would do if alone.

3. Pause and complete a full breath cycle.

4. Now start at the top of the mirror and slowly scan your body from head to toe, while slowly counting to ten.

5. Reverse this process, scanning from the bottom to the top, while slowly counting to ten.

6. Pause, breathe, and look again at yourself in the mirror—as a whole.

7. Process your experience and discuss with peers. What is the difference in the way you initially viewed yourself vs. this scanning approach? Review Question 2 for more assistance in processing.

★ REVIEW GUIDANCE: This task is not to encourage "mirror usage," compartmentalizing or filtering. Remind the clients of the importance of connecting to their inner bodily experiences as a way of living in their body, not via mirrors, apps, or other external means.

Experiential Task 4 BODY TRACING/MAPPING

This exercise aids in clarifying one's perception and/or perceptual distortion.

> **PREP:** A client who willingly trusts the others in this group chooses to be traced standing or lying down, and the group agrees to respond genuinely.

> **PROPS:** Large sheet of paper taped on floor or wall for tracing client, and three markers in varying colors

TASK: Group Body Tracing

1. The chosen client (you) is traced carefully by a friend or therapist your choice. The tracer uses a colored marker and is careful not to tilt the marker in or out, but rather to hold it straight. Once the tracing is completed and deemed satisfactory, you share it with your group members. The group then decides if it is "accurate" (a touch-up may be required). The drawing is then presented to you by the group as your "accurate" image.

> GUIDANCE: This is time for all to pause (thirty to sixty seconds) and stay present as you view your "accurate" image. No discussion takes place yet.

2. You now trace over that drawing with an outline of your "perception" using a marker in a different color. You present it to the group.

> GUIDANCE: This is time for all to pause to take in and comprehend your "perception." No discussion takes place yet.

3. You now trace your "ideal /goal" image over the other tracings with a marker in another color.

> GUIDANCE: This is time to pause with others to take in what you desire.

4. Now it is time to discuss with your group the difference between your "perception," your "ideal/goal," and your "accurate" tracings. Discuss any level of danger in striving for your "ideal" image. Note question 7 for information on the dangers of seeking an ideal image.

5. If you wish, add words inside your drawing to describe your inner traits.

6. You now look at it all—the culmination of subjective and objective self.

> GUIDANCE: Pause, breath, and take it all in.

7. Allow time for all to share feelings and thoughts of the process.

Experiential Task 5 BODY SCHEMA DRAWING

Body schema is "a pattern of awareness leading to basic core assumptions of body and self." (Oxford Dictionary, 1987, p. 846). It is concretized via these drawings. Your drawing creates a means for you to investigate your body attitudes—both positive and negative. There are three versions of this exercise.

PROPS: A drawing of a body in contour (I borrowed from Whole Person Press, 1996—this works well, as it is an average-size body) and fine-point markers in various colors.

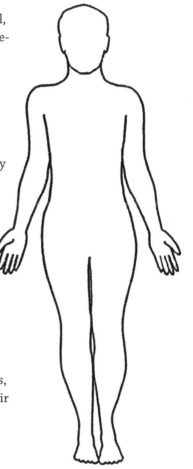

TASK: Individual Body Schema Drawing (Version I)

1. Encourage participants to think of experiences and memories they have of their body.

2. Draw inside or outside of the contour any of your feelings, experiences, opinions.

3. After completing the drawing, share the symbols, colors, and words you used to describe yourself.

4. Encourage clients to provide feedback and discussion surrounding the symbols, designs, color choices, and meaning of their drawing.

TASK: Individual Body Schema (Version II)

1. Encourage clients to think of experiences and memories they have of their body.

2. Write inside or outside any words describing feelings or experiences related to their body. Important: each participant uses only one marker.

3. Process notations with clients to explore their commonly held attitudes and beliefs.

TASK: Group Body Schema (Version III)

PREP: Use the above-mentioned drawing, complete with feelings, comments, and opinions, and write your initials at the top of your page. Important: every participant chooses one marker, a different color for everyone, to use throughout the task.

1. Pass the drawing to the person to your left. Write feedback/comments.

2. After two or three minutes, pass again to your left. Write feedback/comments.

3. Continue passing to each person until the drawing returns to its owner.

4. Spend a few minutes looking over your drawing and the comments.

5. Individually, share the pieces and resultant feelings. Process the importance of receiving a compliment or feedback. Why is it difficult to accept feedback? Encourage accepting and letting in. Experiential Task 7 will be helpful with this.

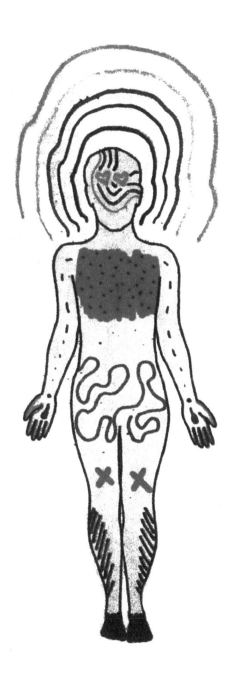

Example of individual body schema (Version 1)

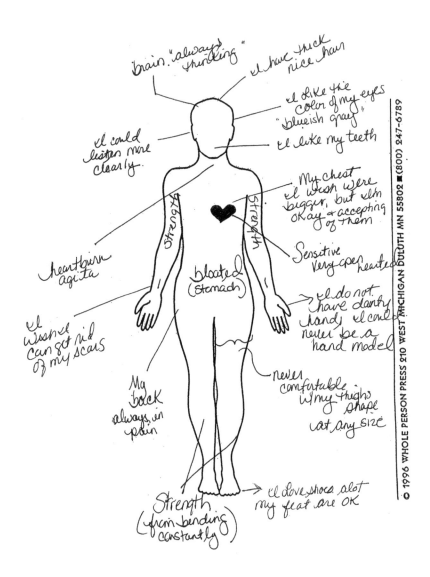

brain "always thinking"

I have thick nice hair

I Like the color of my eyes "blueish gray"

I could listen more clearly.

I like my teeth

My chest I wish were bigger, but I'm OKay + accepting of them

Strength

Strength

Sensitive very open hearted

heartburn agita

bloated (Stomach)

I do not have dainty hands, I could never be a hand model

I wished I can get rid of my scars

My back always in pain

never comfortable w/my thighs shape at any size

Strength (from bending constantly)

I love shoes alot my feat are OK

© 1996 WHOLE PERSON PRESS 210 WEST MICHIGAN DULUTH MN 55802 ■ (800) 247-6789

Example of individual body schema (Version II)

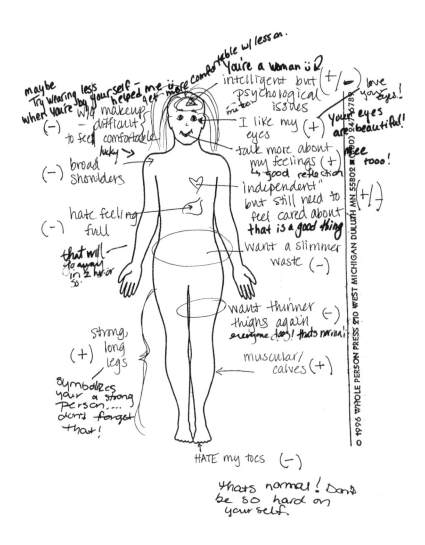

Example of Group body schema (Version III)

GETTING BACK TO YOU

Experiential Task 6 FINDING YOUR RAINBOW

A popular style of "distorted thinking" identified by Albert Ellis in 1955 is also known as polarized thinking—black or white, good or bad, all or nothing. Clients who struggle with body image dissatisfaction tend to state: "I have to be perfect-looking or I am a failure." Many struggle with food and weight issues—eating disorders, yo-yo dieting, going from one extreme to the other.

Although "black-and-white thinking" serves a purpose for finding facts, it does not aid in emotional situations. "Rainbow thinking" is more flexible and open, allowing for more possibilities and perspectives. The rainbow is the in-between, the middle ground flanked by two extreme styles of thinking. Finding this spot will help you find options and possibilities in problem-solving, leading to greater perseverance and far less self-sabotaging. I learned of "rainbow thinking" in the late 1990s while attending an eating-disorder conference in Massachusetts held by MEDA. Although the origin of the concept is unclear, its usage has spread far and wide.

Example of black /rainbow/white thinking:

All	*Some*	*None*
Always	*Sometimes*	*Never*
Good	*OK*	*Bad*
Rich	*Average*	*Poor*

PROPS: Colored markers and paper

TASK:

1. On a sheet of paper, list your black/white styles of thinking.

2. Now, place your own middle style of thinking. This middle style is the rainbow between the black-and-white extreme thinking.

3. Discuss how the middle feels, rather than the extreme.

GUIDANCE: Aim for personal and specific topics. "What about food?" "Body?" "Perfection?" Following the written task, try making "I statements" using the rainbow style. E.g., "I am learning."

Fat	Average	Skinny
Perfect	Okay	Flawed
Success	Learning	Failure

Experiential Task 7 TAKING A COMPLIMENT

When a compliment is heard, it may bring up a "boundary disturbance," producing "anxiety related to self-consciousness, fear of exposure, and fear of allowing others emotionally or physically close" (Young, 1995). This exercise is devised to assist one in accepting a compliment and improving self-esteem.

Following is a list of " Four Levels to Accepting a Compliment," created by clients in my private practice, BI Group.

1. Denying the compliment: Saying, "No, it's not really true." (rejecting the compliment)

2. Acknowledging you heard it: Responding, "I heard it, but..." (not able to believe the person or the compliment).

3. Acknowledging the compliment: Replying "thank you." (allowing for another's perception even though you do not believe it).

4. Acknowledging you received the compliment: Replying "OMG, thank you." (believing that a compliment might be true).

> GUIDANCE: Discuss the varying levels between fully accepting a compliment and rejecting a compliment (partially or fully).

PROPS: Pencil, marker, and paper for each participant.

TASK: Drawing the Boundary

1. With a pencil, draw the boundary between you and the person giving you the compliment. What would it be made of? Would it be glass, straw, concrete, wood, barbed wire, brick, etc.?

2. Would there be an opening?

3. Could the payer of compliments come in? See in? Can you see out?

4. How permanent is this material? Can it ever change? When? How?

5. Do you have a boundary disturbance? E.g. when people give you a compliment, is there a fear of dependency? Is this drawing representative of a fear of dependency?

★ *GUIDANCE FOR THERAPISTS: Do not be surprised if this drawing indicates an impermeable material such as concrete or cement. The image or scene may be located in a remote place, such as the top of a mountain or in a thick forest. Explore the symbolic meaning of the choice of material, location, climate, etc. Remember, the choices represent a boundary that serves as a protection from trusting others (e.g., fear of losing autonomy, denial of suppressed needs). Refer to Question 16, Task 14, and the glossary for information on "boundary disturbance."*

Experiential Task 8 TRASH 'EM!

This exercise is for those who rely on rituals, patterns, or habits related to disordered eating and body image dissatisfaction.

PROP: A trash barrel to place in the middle of the group circle formation.

PREP: Search around your home or vehicle for objects that fuel or represent your eating disorder or negative body image. Some examples are concrete, such as clothing that no longer fits and is unrealistic to keep. Other examples are symbolic, such as a clock to represent all the time spent on body image and eating behavior rituals. Ask yourself if you can entertain the idea of trashing that piece as a symbol of change. If you feel strongly connected to it and still rely on it, move onto another object that you can let go of at this point in your recovery.

In a recent "Trash 'Em" session I watched a client trash her pageant heels and accompanying costume jewelry used in past swimsuit contests. Her stated reason to dispose of these items was based on her desire to let go of negative body thoughts and obsessions, which stem from years of pageant competition in which her body was viewed, judged, and critiqued. How exciting to witness such a brave act indicating her newly empowered sense of self. Brava!

PREP: Cover all numbers or labels with tape so as to not "trigger" anyone. (See also Questions 6 and 7 and glossary for info on triggers.)

TASK:

1. One person at a time shares the purpose and meaning of the chosen object and why they have a desire to let go of it (e.g., jeans that don't fit, obsession with thighs, etc.).

2. They now "take back" something to replace that object (e.g., strong legs).

3. They trash the article in the barrel (a round of applause is appropriate here).

4. Following the completion of all trashings, the group goes out to a dumpster to trash everything into it (a round of applause is encouraged here).

Experiential Task 9 YOGA THEORY
AND PRACTICE FOR POSITIVE BODY IMAGE

Positive body image requires self-nurturing or caring for body, mind, and spirit equally. Christina Sell's book *Yoga from the Inside Out: Making Peace with Your Body Through Yoga* stresses the importance of "self-inquiry" and "practicing being in relationship with our bodies." The act of following the breath entering the body increases awareness of self-perception. This way to "monitor the criticisms and judgments" allows you to begin healing through nonjudgmental awareness while simultaneously decreasing self-objectification. You replace that self-objectification with an "increase in kinesthetic awareness and responsiveness to your bodily sensations" (Sell, 2003, pp. 51–53).

A study in *Psychology of Women Quarterly* reports that "yoga is associated with greater body satisfaction and fewer symptoms of eating disorders than traditional forms of aerobic exercise like jogging or cardio machines." The greater the number of hours a woman practiced yoga in a week the less likely she was to suffer self-objectification and the more likely she was to be satisfied with her body, while the more hours a woman spent performing aerobic activity the greater the link to disordered eating. "In yoga class, a woman develops sensitivity to bodily sensations and practices listening to her body's feedback" (Daubenmier, 2005).

To achieve the many benefits of yoga you must integrate yoga into your life. Erich Schiffmann states: "Never underestimate the importance of balance, strength and flexibility. These physical benefits of yoga practice accrue from a regular practice. On the mat one faces their body with all their doubts, criticisms and comparative thinking. One is left to work with the unknown part of themselves as they explore new uncharted territory" (1996, p. 24). This yogic path or practice becomes a way for you to disentangle your resistance. This sounds hard, but it can also feel good to experience yourself in this new way. Difficult as it may be for you to stand up and face your life situation, it can actually be pleasurable to move. Alexander Lowen's theory of pleasure explains that sensory impressions connect to matching rhythms inside oneself. "The pleasure is rhythm and rhythm brings us pleasure because pleasure is the perception of rhythmical flow of excitement in the body" (Lowen, 1993).

Yoga has relaxing benefits as well. The slow quality of breath activates the parasympathetic system—the part of your nervous system that tells your muscles to relax. Its important function helps you to sleep better, helps your digestion, and builds your immune system. (This is not true for power or vigorous yoga, but rather for a regulated yoga style whereby breathing is synchronized with movement in a slow relaxed manner.) Yoga is not about being perfect or driven, as it supports wherever we are. Whereas eating-disorder clients tend to emphasize appearance and believe their self-worth is based on their body and appearance, yoga is there to build self-trust, nonjudgmental styles of thinking. The journey inward begins through the practice of asanas (poses), pranayama (breathing techniques), meditation, and relaxation. Yoga, as a tool for change and acceptance, builds self-tolerance and helps you allow for accepting life on life's terms—rather than on your terms. You will realize that the result or outcome of our changing, controlling, and managing life is not in your hands, and that can bring a feeling of relief and "letting go." This letting go is not the same as resigning or giving up on change. It is actually crucial to successful and lasting change as it works from a base of knowledge, acceptance, and clarity, which allow you to see what and who you really are—without lingering misconceptions.

Surya Namaskara (Sun Salutation)

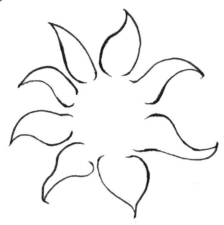

TASK: Surya Namaskara (Sun Salutation)

GUIDANCE: When folding over or bending, use the exhalation with the flow of movement. When stretching or lengthening, use the inhalation with the flow of movement. When twisting, use the exhalation with the flow of movement. In all cases, the breath and the movement are one and the same— supporting each other (Schiffmann, 1996, pp. 57–58).

PROPS: Yoga mat, comfortable clothing, and space to move in

1. Stand in standing pose (Tadasana) with hands in prayer position (Anjali mudra).

2. As you stretch your arms up, breathe in, touching your hands at the top of your in-breath (Full Tadasana).

3. As you exhale, bend forward with arms coming down to the earth (Modified Uttanasana).

4. Inhale, extending your right leg straight back, bending your left knee over the heel of that foot into a lunge, with your hands placed on the earth.

5. Exhale, extending your left leg back to meet your right. Hold in plank (Phalakasana).

6. Engage your abdominal muscles as you gradually lower down to the floor in one solid plank-like piece (Chaturanga Dandasana).

7. Breathe in while pressing hips down through legs, lifting up from the crown of your head into a back bend (Bhujangasana).

8. Exhale, lifting back into a reversed "V" shape—leading with navel to tailbone high up, hips high and back, with arms lined diagonally from wrists to elbows to shoulders to hips and heels working toward the earth (Adho Mukha Svanasana).

9. Breathe in, looking forward between your hands, and exhale while sweeping your right leg up to the right hand, with knee bending over that foot into lunge.

10. Inhale and, with an exhalation, bring the back foot forward to meet the right with hands to the earth (Modified Utanasana).

11. Inhale, lifting your arms and hands above to touch at the top of your in-breath while standing (Full Tadasana).

12. Exhale while returning your hands to prayer position (Anjali mudra) at your heart–still standing (Tadasana).

13. Pause and repeat entire sequence on your left side.

14. Following the completion of Surya Namaskara, remain in Tadasana; bring one hand to your heart and the other hand to your chest or abdomen, taking time to notice your heart beat and breath working together. Remain for one minute—present in the moment of noticing with your full awareness as you explore the dynamic energy in stillness.

15. End with hands in prayer position (Anjali Mudra) stating "Namaste," which means "from the good in me to the good in you."

Practicing Yogic Reality

There is much more to yogic philosophy than I can touch on, yet one principal yogic philosophical approach encourages noticing the way we see and perceive things, believing that thoughts create the reality we live in. With a "yogic mind" (buddhi) one learns the mind is the intelligence of our heart, and practicing how to develop this yogic mind comes through inner knowledge and meditation. The belief is that we choose our thoughts and our reality, and that it is possible to re-create our styles of thinking. We simply ask the old thoughts to step aside as we try on new thoughts. The focus is on positive thinking, the practice of seeing good in all—therefore creating a positive reality in which to experience yourself and all beings.

TASK: Practicing Yogic Thinking

When creating new thoughts, be careful not to use words such as "should," "ought to," "can't," "won't," and any rigid, absolute styles. Keep your positive thoughts in the present tense.

1. Practice standing in mountain pose (tadasana), shifting your weight between both feet, deepening while lifting into balance and alignment.

2. Say "I am," allowing the pose and the words to reinforce each other.

3. Practice saying one of these: "I am worthy." "I am loving." "I eat well, exercise, and rest well to enjoy my health."

4. Find a statement to fit your needs. Practice saying it out loud to another. Write it down on paper to remember. Embrace it!

During this time of change and fluctuation you may feel more uncertain as to exactly who you are. This may feel strange. This could account for the change of your old self for a newer self. Temporarily uprooted, soon to be grounded, growing with balance—lifting upward while rooting downward. The symbol of the lotus flower exemplifies this.

"With its root in the mud, the lotus flower raises itself through the muddy water to reveal its beauty floating clearly on the water's surface." The flower symbolizes the "rising of the soul from a confusing place to one of enlightenment." (Turlington, 2002).

Yoga Mudras

Mudras are the bridge between one's spiritual experience and one's interactions with the world. They are known as "prayers translated into physical form."

PREP: In a comfortable seated position (Sukhasana or Virasana), create these gestures with your hands, naming each one along with its intention, connecting heart and mind.

TASK:

1. *Anjali Mudra* (prayer pose): often accompanied by the word "Namaste."

2. *Chin Mudra* (unites opposite pose): with open palm placed on knee; may add tip of index finger meeting tip of thumb. This invites energy of others in (while palms facing down on knees forms a closed energy circuit to contain your own energy).

3. *Padma Mudra* (lotus seal): with heels of the palms together, thumbs touching, keep knuckles separate and fingers blossoming. Experience the heart opening.

4. *Wheel of Dharma* (truth poses): with thumbs to index fingertips, left middle fingertip to right thumb.

5. *Samadhi Mudra* (non-separateness pose): interlock fingers. Index fingers point up with thumb tips touching.

6. *Abhaya Mudra* (fearless pose): One arm is lifted at shoulder height, palm facing forward while the other hand is placed on thigh facing downward.

The Five Principles of Yoga
to be incorporated into our daily lives:

1. Relaxation

2. Asanas

3. Breathing

4. Proper diet

5. Meditation and positive thinking

Experiential Task 10 FINDING STILLNESS

The words of Erich Schiffmann guide us:

> *Yoga is a way of moving into stillness in order to experience the*
> *truth of who you are. What does it feel like to be relaxed, calm*
> *and quiet inside? It's about being still in the moment you are*
> *present in. For a few minutes, every form of external activity*
> *stops. Then, in quietness you turn your attention toward and*
> *focus on yourself. Focus on what it feels like to be you. When*
> *you let go of everything you think you know about yourself*
> *and stay with what is left. When you willingly abandon the*
> *contradictory evaluations of who you are and courageously*
> *reach deeply into yourself you will come to a new experience*
> *of who you are…you will sense the creative energy that is*
> *the creative life of you. You will then define and think about*
> *yourself in a new and expanded way. This is central to your*
> *perception, behavior and experience of you are. (1996, p. 4)*

This may be very scary for those with negative body image thoughts, feelings, and sensations. Being present is what many avoid as the mind latches onto unresolved thoughts from the past or anticipatory thoughts of the unknown future. No worries. Start here—where you are. Follow your guiding breath at all times, returning to it as an anchor, securing you in this present place of refuge and safety. You can move into stillness as you find balance in a standing pose. This becomes a metaphor for your life, your daily shifting, struggles, and imbalanced times, as you realign yourself.

Vrikshasana (Tree Pose)

TASK: Tree Pose (Vrikshasana)

1. Stand in mountain pose and shift your weight to one side until you have distributed your weight equally between both feet.

2. Shift your weight to one side and bend the opposite leg lifting your foot to knee Balance as you notice how your body is rooted into the earth, yet at the same time it is growing toward the heavens— lifted up above.

3. Create a "two directional line of energy" (Schiffmann, 1996, p. 45) as you energetically deepen downward through the standing leg while simultaneously lifting from your center upward.

4. Hold the pose by staying with your breath in stillness. Explore shifting from thoughts of the past or future worries back to the present breath.

This simple standing pose will stabilize you and reaffirm your existence in this moment. Each time you become aware of simply standing you have the opportunity to bring attention to your body supported by the earth beneath you—lifted toward the heavens above us. Finding your alignment, balance, and a stillness within yourself will organize you in a new way and shed a similar effect on our thinking and feeling. The powerful truth that movement has a corresponding effect on how you think and feel is one of the principle theories in movement therapy. Stillness also has a corresponding effect on how we think and feel, as stillness is a balanced, dynamic kind of movement.

Yoga Meditation

TASK: Yoga Meditation

PROP: A rolled-up blanket or pillow underneath your "ischial tuberosity bones" or "sits bones," a chime or bell, and 10 minutes of undisturbed time

1. Sit in either seated (Sukhasana) or kneeling (Vajrasana) pose.

2. Look downward or close eyes.

3. Take a moment to "arrive" here in this present moment.

4. Physically as well arrive here by connecting with the earth beneath you. Do this from your center, rooting down from your tail bone and your sits bones toward the earth.

5. From center now lengthen upward toward the heavens as you lift to separate between each vertebra.

6. With this alignment of rooted and lifted come home by bringing your attention inwardly to your breath.

7. Follow your breath with the rise of each in-breath.

8. Follow your breath with the fall of each out-breath.

9. Let your breath guide you as you follow this wave of your breath.

10. When/if your mind wanders, notice this and let your thought go—like a cloud passing by.

11. Return back to your breath again...and again...and again if your mind wanders.

12. Stay with your breath; immerse yourself in your breathing, finding a rhythm for a few minutes

13. Let the slow rhythm of your exhalations carry you deeper down into a place of stillness.

14. Immerse yourself in your breathing on your own, now for a few more minutes.

15. At the sound of the bell, return your attention back to the room.

16. Open your eyes as you breathe in and exhale.

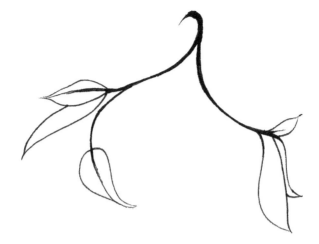

Experiential Task 11 COMING HOME TO CENTER

We lose our connection from our inner guidance, intuition, inner voice, or "center" when we are thrown off balance by addictions such as eating disorders, shopping sprees, gambling, working overtime, etc. These compulsions and obsessions destroy our connection to our inner world by making us more concerned with what is "out there" and less concerned with what is "in here."

TASK: Finding Center

1. Allow yourself time to become quiet...

2. Turn your attention inward...

3. Let your thoughts drift away like clouds softly scooting across the sky...

4. Take a deep breath...and exhale slowly...letting tension leave your body and drift away with the wind...leaving you relaxed...and quiet...

5. Focus on your breathing...hearing yourself breathe in deeply and out again...with a sigh. Pause five seconds

6. Allow yourself to stay focused on this moment...

7. If your mind wanders simply notice it happening...

8. Gently pull your attention back...to this time with yourself...and the rhythm of your breathing. Pause five seconds.

9. Take a deep breath in...

10. Where does the deepest breath reach?...

11. Touch this place now...and gently pat...this center of your life force...

12. Using your "inner voice" say "I am me" several times slowly...

13. Point to this place...

14. Where do you point?...

15. Touch the place that is you and gently massage this spot... the center of your being...

16. Notice that you may have several centers...they all are valid...and true for you....

17. Take time now to select the one...that feels best to you...

18. Choose the space...where you can be yourself...know yourself...and love yourself...

19. Trust yourself to find your center...which holds your truth... and the wisdom...the source of your light...and energy...and life.

20. Keep your hand on this special place...while you prepare to return to your surroundings...secure in knowing that you can find this place again...anytime...anywhere...you need it...

21. When you are ready...slowly turn your attention to the room and rejoin the group...feeling centered with yourself and others in the room...maintaining the balance you found...in your body. Pause five seconds. (Adapted from Ryan & Travis, 1991)

Experiential Task 12 THE POWER OF ONE'S BREATH

Our breathing will react to anything that affects us and therefore will change with our emotional states: a moment of joy, of stress, of fear. Our breath adjusts to the needs that arise in that moment—it may be staccato and choppy or fluid and steady. However, we can learn to use our breath more effectively and efficiently during stressful times, regulating our emotions by slowing down our exhalation. Using the power of a longer exhalation engages your parasympathetic system to work with your central nervous system—slowing your rapid heartbeat and relieving your anxious state. Herbert Benson at the Institute for Mind Body Medicine at Harvard University studied these benefits with his "relaxation response," whereby lowering the heart rate and breathing rate created a state of mental calmness (Benson & Klipper, 1976). Stephen Cope, a psychotherapist, educator, and senior yoga instructor, writes and teaches on contemporary psychology and Eastern traditions. His "riding the wave of breath" technique is fully described in *Yoga and the Quest for the True Self* (2000). The five stages of his simple practice help to integrate the physical and emotional with the energy from breathing. They are breathe, relax, feel, watch, and allow. This in-depth look into breathing can help enlighten those who have lost their connection to the world of sensations and body.

The breathing tasks below are more simplified versions to explore. These are expanded upon in numerous books devoted to yoga and pranayama (breath control).

PROPS: A rolled-up blanket, mat, or pillow to sit on

> GUIDANCE: Pause and reflect on the tone you use when you assist another in a breathing task.

CORRECT BREATHING

1. Place hands on your abdomen, fingers touching.

2. Breathe in and feel the expansion of the lower abdomen, diaphragm, and chest, noticing how your hands separate.

3. Breathe out as you feel the contraction of chest, diaphragm, and abdomen, noticing how your hands return.

4. Repeat this two or three times as you close your eyes and experience your new breathing pattern.

THE WAVE BREATH

To deepen your awareness of your breathing.

1. Place your right hand on your heart and your left on your abdomen.

2. Start with the exhalation—letting as much air out as you comfortably can.

3. Breathe in, filling up your abdomen first, your diaphragm second, and then your chest. Notice the sequential expansion like a wave, feeling your left hand rise, and your right hand expand with your ribs.

4. Exhale—releasing first from the chest, next from your diaphragm, and lastly your abdomen—witnessing a sequential fading away of the wave breath.

5. Repeat with eyes closed, staying with your sensations of each breath flowing in and each breath flowing out.

6. Notice how this breath cycle continues without directing the breath for three or four complete wave breath sequences

RATIO BREATHING: To sooth your nervous system

1. Start with four steady counts of in-breaths.

2. Balance these using four steady counts of out-breaths.

3. Repeat with four counts in—pause one count—and five counts out.

4. Repeat with four counts in—pause one count—and six counts out.

5. Repeat with four counts in—pause one count—and seven counts out.

6. Repeat with four counts in—pause one count—and eight counts out.

7. Notice your breath pattern continues naturally with longer exhalations, and how relaxed you can feel from this 2 to 1 breathing ratio.

UJJAYI BREATHING (VICTORIOUS BREATH): To enliven yoga poses

1. Begin with balanced breathing: four counts in and four counts out.

2. Breathe in through your nostrils toward the back of your throat with your mouth closed while tightening around the opening of your windpipe.

3. Exhale from the back of your throat with the sound of "ah" with your mouth closed.

4. Repeat this with awareness of the soft, deep, yet hollow sound coming with a vibration from the back of your throat.

ALTERNATE NOSTRIL BREATHING: To relieve tension headaches and open sinus passages.

PREP: Sit comfortably, with back straight yet relaxed.

> GUIDANCE: For best results, match counts for inhalations and exhalations within a round. Practice lengthening the counts with each round.

1. Place RIGHT thumb on nostril and fourth finger near left nostril.
2. Close the RIGHT nostril and inhale deeply through left nostril.
3. Release the RIGHT nostril, close LEFT, and exhale through the RIGHT.
4. Keeping LEFT nostril closed, inhale deeply.
5. Close RIGHT nostril and exhale out completely.
6. Repeat pattern five to ten cycles.
7. Add ratio breaths with each cycle.

EMOTIONAL BREATHING

1. Repeat yoga meditation (Task 10, steps 1–10)

2. Shift your focus to what you are experiencing on an emotional level.

3. Notice what feelings come up.

4. Do not label the feelings—just notice them. Perhaps more than one will surface.

5. Do not identify with the feelings. They are just "states of being." Acknowledge them as feelings.

6. Inhale, coming back to the breath, and when you exhale, notice you tolerated the feeling by breathing with it.

7. Repeat for three complete breath cycles, staying with your breath and immersing yourself in your breathing. The only reality is now, here in this moment.

8. Feel what it is like to live in the present moment, breathing in and out. For now, the present moment is one breath in and one breath out. Remain here for 5 mins.

9. Wiggle your toes and fingers, stretching out.

10. Come back with eyes open to the room.

HARD WORK PAYS OFF

Experiential Task 13 PEELING THE ONION

Our focus on eating-disorder symptoms brings attention to the surface of an eating disorder but often neglects the underlying issues, which require treatment for a full recovery. Body image issues left unaddressed will lead again and again to an eating disorder. Tolerating the barrage of negative styles of thinking that accompany body image dissatisfaction and distortion, such as "good or bad/all or nothing" judging of your body, the "not good enough/perfectionistic" style of criticism, and fear-based "catastrophic thinking" can be unbearable. Indeed, each of these styles is burdensome on its own, but the effect is amplified when they are combined.

A person subject to these styles will likely end up at risk in the jungle of eating disorders as the body becomes the culprit and bearer of these attacks, blamed for its imperfections and betrayals and leading one to seek drastic approaches to body changes. Thoughts, feelings, and behaviors need to be examined to prevent further symptoms.

In *Effective Clinical Practice in the Treatment of Eating Disorders,* Robin Sesan reminds us as therapists to assist clients in identifying what is "unforgivable" (2009, p. 244). This process reminds me of the metaphor of peeling an onion, one layer at a time, as we work deeper into what drives clients' negative thoughts toward their body. The act of peeling an onion is painful and difficult to endure. As each layer is peeled away, a "sting" surfaces—a feeling of self-hatred, shame, or guilt, for example. Frequently I hear "disgusting," "gross," "fat," "selfish," or other harsh self-talk words. These hurts pile up, constructing a belief that one will "never be good enough" and therefore never lovable. Experiencing the sting may bring on frustration, and the deeper work may be avoided at all costs. However, it is here where compassion toward oneself becomes possible. Only by peeling the layers away and working toward what is underneath will one connect with basic human needs. This opens the prison door, freeing a long-lost part of oneself. Should powerful negative emotions resurface, direct your client to the breath and stay with the breath to ground the body and remain present. In completing a breath cycle one has tolerated "the sting" and is closer to recognizing disowned emotion as "humanness." Continue with another breath cycle. Staying with the sensations of the breath one can experience the reality—"now"—and what it feels like to be present with one's emotions. Gradually, while staying present with the breath and "riding the wave" of emotions, without judgment, one can allow acceptance toward the "burdened" or "unforgivable" self. This targets the "relationship between emotion and body image" and can "break the cycle of perceived threat and reaction to body image, including reactive behaviors that confirm the perceived threat" (Williamson, Stewart, White, & York-Crowe, 2004, p. 53). The impetus and tendency to self-judge will dissipate through many breath cycles, as the human need to be loved and the basic right to be safe surfaces. Remember, it is the breath working its power: inhalation aids in the tolerance of these intense feelings, and exhalation allows one to stay present long enough to feel the lessening of the ebb and flow with each intense wave of feelings. "Recovery is about opening up to life—the good and the bad, and living with a more open heart. It is through the practice of forgiveness and the accompanying skills that we learn to transform anger and shame into compassion and love for ourselves and others" (Sesan, 2009, p. 235).

Peace within makes beauty without.

· English Proverb ·

TASK: Peeling Layers and Layers

Ask client to:

1. Identify the feeling from an upsetting situation.

2. When you feel that feeling, what else do you feel?

3. When you feel that way, how do you feel inside?

4. What is the underlying feeling you have of yourself when you feel that way?

5. Feeling that way leads to what else?

6. What need do you have at this time to help you?

7. Take a moment to imagine your need being met.

In peeling the onion, with each layer we come to another feeling that brings us closer to an unmet need. Using the task above I guided a young adult client in my Women's Body Image/Self Care Group through the process. Her peeling process was witnessed by other group participants. With her permission, I now share her words: "I feel shame at the doctor's office...When I feel shame, I feel lonely... when I feel lonely, I feel unlovable...when I feel unlovable, I feel like a bad person. That makes me feel unworthy or not good enough." Connecting to the deep "bud" of the onion, I posed the question: "What do you need?" "What I need is a friend to listen and validate I am okay." A moment of acknowledging her "humanness" is spent in the session. Participants often share how those feelings and emotions resonate with them as well.

★ *FOLLOW-UP GUIDANCE: It can be helpful for the client to journal and process throughout the week, noticing any emotional or behavioral impact that arises with this experience.*

TASK: Clustering

In a group therapy session, it is not uncommon for a participant to state he/she wants to let go of old hurts, indicating they are ready to peel away some layers. Using a different approach, this simple task—adapted from "clustering," a technique created by Gabriele Rico (2000)—will assist in unblocking stuck or immobilized feelings. We find that this expressive/creative art therapy technique is more immediate and direct than verbal therapy, as it is effective in rediscovering lost spontaneity.

PROPS: Paper and markers

1. In the center of a piece of paper, draw a circle.

2. In the circle write a word that represents a feeling or mood—something present in your life (i.e., trait or feeling).

3. Draw five or six lines from the circle to make what look like rays from the sun.

4. On each line write another word that you associate with the circled word. Think fast, no censoring.

5. Write a sentence, story, or short paragraph using all of these words.

6. Share your writing with the group.

Clustering Poems

These are clustering poems created by clients.

TRUST

Trust is when you are taking a risk.
You are sharing a part of yourself that you are letting go of
TRUST is having faith
And believing in someone that you are relying on.

STOMACH

I feel sad because I feel fat and that feeling to me is gross.
I don't like that my stomach is big and pudgy.
I feel like this all the time-always have and am afraid
I always will.

FORGIVENESS

Unless I release the blame I hold toward you, I will not be free
from my self-blame and I will continue to suffer the hurt you
have caused me.

★ *FOLLOW-UP GUIDANCE: Experiential therapies may resurrect intense feelings. Clients will ask, "How do I understand where to go from here?" This is an appropriate question, as negative feelings and emotions have surfaced. How does the healing take place?*

There is no simple answer, as each person's needs depend on his or her present life situation. Therefore, I have found different tasks click for different people, and often this is in the presence of others who "witness" the process—offering a validation to the client. The below is an example of a soothing task to calm one following emotional depth in a session.

TASK: Color Prism Journey

EXAMPLE: Soothing "color prism"

1. Find a comfortable place in a room where you are relaxed. Spend a minute finding your breath.

2. Follow your exhalation down into a place of stillness. Pause and relax. Allow yourself to use your imagination to bring each color I mention into your mind—seeing its properties and qualities.

3. Start with the color PINK, which symbolizes love, closeness, compassion, caring, and passion. Imagine these attributes in this color.

4. Moving through the prism, we come into the color CORAL, which represents courage to love again, intimacy, and relationships. Let this color and its qualities be present in your mind and body now.

5. Flowing through CORAL we reach the color ORANGE. ORANGE embraces life, moving on from the past. Allow this color to radiate throughout your mind in this present moment.

6. We move through the prism, coming into GOLD. This is congruent with knowing yourself, discernment and wisdom. See it's illuminating quality as you relax.

7. YELLOW is inside the prism as we travel onward. Self-esteem, fun, and laughter come with the joyful tone of YELLOW. Feel the vibrancy of yellow's aspects.

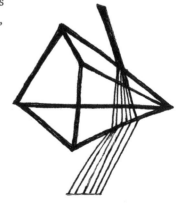

8. The rainbow of prism colors blend into GREEN, where decisions and choices, balance and emotions reside. Settle into this color with its many hues and tones.

9. Flow now into the color TURQUOISE, where creativity, freedom, individuality, and playfulness come forth. Allow the feeling tone of TURQUOISE to permeate all your senses.

10. Our prism journey now continues into the color BLUE. Find your own healing shade of blue where peace, trust, speaking your mind, and authority exist. How many shades of blue do you know? What characteristics do you associate with each?

11. VIOLET now comes forth with its properties of imagination, deeper beliefs about life, and transformation. Known also for a future vision, we picture this color to sense its unique quality and distinction.

12. This prism journey brings us into the ending color, known as MAGENTA—loving every moment, caring for humanity and other living creatures. Let the color MAGENTA be vivid in your mind's eye for a few seconds as it deeply resonates.

13. Take a moment to pause and gradually return your attention to the room.

14. Discuss: What colors do you prefer? Do you have a favorite color or one you tend to enjoy more than other colors, one that resonated with you? Do any colors stimulate awareness of a quality within yourself? Which colors calm or sooth you? (Adapted from Dalichow, 1996)

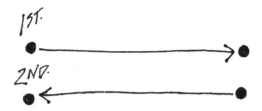

Experiential Task 14 SETTING HEALTHY BOUNDARIES

This task can help to clarify how to set boundaries with others if you tend to "people-please" and/or "approval-seek."

TASK 1: Learning to Set Boundaries

PREP: Begin with participants on either side of the room facing each other. On one side are "the doers." Across from them are "the receivers." The doers go first. As always, it is important to prepare by finding one's breath and becoming grounded kinesthetically.

1. Establish a grounding position such as Mountain Pose (Tadasana). Locate the breath. Follow the breath and stay inside, locating "center" before you begin.

2. Instruct your clients: "When you feel the impetus to move, walk toward the person in front of you and stop where you feel comfortably stopping."

3. Note the place where one stops and validate the choice. "This is where you have stopped. Is this correct?"

4. Explore the impetus behind the decision to stop, asking: "Are you comfortable with your choice?"

5. "What made you choose to stop here?" For some the answer is, "I don't want to be closer." For others it is, "I didn't want to stop here, but I thought I would insult him/her if I stopped any closer or further away than I did."

6. Did you respond from your center? Or defer to the others need?

7. Reverse roles so that "the doers" become "the receivers" and "the receivers" become "the doers."

8. Repeat steps.

> GUIDANCE: In processing this task, remind participants that the task was not to teach about others' needs or comfort zone. "The task was to strengthen your confidence in setting a boundary based on your (not their) comfort zone." They may say, "I am not comfortable if they are not comfortable." Remind them to focus on themselves and avoid co-dependency. We learn from trial and error that the way to the center is through the self, honoring your intuition and "inner voice."

TASK 2: Learning to Set limits

PREP: In this version of the task, "the doer" walks up to "the receiver," and "the receiver" says "STOP" whenever he/she feels the need to.

Again, begin with participants on either side of the room facing each other. On one side are "the doers." Across from them are "the receivers." The doers go first.

1. Establish a grounding position such as Mountain Pose (Tadasana). Locate the breath.

2. Follow the breath and stay inside, locating "center" before beginning to move.

3. Instruct the receivers: "When the doers begin toward you, and come to a place you are comfortable with them being, say "stop." Validate the receiver's choice: "This is where you have said to stop. Is this correct?"

4. Explore their impetus behind the decision to say "stop" by asking the receiver: "Are you comfortable with your choice. What made you say "stop" there?"

5. Did you respond from your center? Or did you defer to the other person?

6. Reverse roles and repeat with the same task.

> GUIDANCE: Remember, the task is not to teach people-pleasing or approval-seeking. The task is to learn how to set a boundary and say "stop."

Experiential Task 15 SEEING THROUGH THE MEDIA

Discussing how media messages and images influence our feelings about our body is essential, as your "visual system" will remember images and transfer those images into an "ideal self" in a comparative manner, working against your own body image. These media influences will not cause body image or eating issues, but they can lead to an "internalized ideal image" and unrealistic expectations, setting the stage for body image and food issues. Remember, you alone are the designer and choreographer of your body and your life; your choices create the life you live. Filter the messages of the media (magazine photos, ads, internet photos, Facebook, etc.). Although someone may appear very happy on a page or on a screen, it is an image intended to persuade the consumer to purchase a product.

While leading a body image group in the 1990s I provided each group member a copy of an inspirational reading from *Yoga Journal* magazine. The article focused on breathing as a tool for managing anxiety. We discussed the application of this tool to aid in recovery. It was while doing so that a group participant noted an advertisement on that very page. To my surprise, the ad promoted a diet pill called NoPhedra. Great, I thought...just what we did not need in a treatment program for eating disorders! However, this gave us the opportunity to learn another lesson that day. We learned that an advertisement promoting appetite suppressant products for weight loss could show up in a popular health-oriented magazine. This reinforced a valuable skill—to "filter" media messages in all types of magazines.

TASK: Active advertising Acknowledgment

Discuss the following:

1. What product is this ad promoting?

2. What other messages and feelings are a part of this ad?

3. How did this ad get your attention?

4. Are the people in this ad realistically depicted?

5. Will this ad influence your decision to buy the product?

6. What would you change in the ad if you were in charge? (Borrowed from Maine, 2000, p. 83)

TASK: Letter Writing

1. Identify a leading product that presents unrealistic images of females/males.

2. Send a letter to the company that promotes the product and its advertisement.

3. Explain why it is not helpful to buy into the product.

4. Explain why the image is not helpful to the public.

5. Try not to complain but rather to make suggestions.

6. Ask for a response. (Adapted from Maine, 2000, pp. 100–101)

Here is an example of a letter of concern sent to a local newspaper:

Dear Sir or Madam:

Your March 7th publication displays front-page words "Here's the Skinny" and continues on page 30 with "Skinny Shoreline Chef." The word "skinny" seems harmless to us...but is it? "Skinny" is a loaded word that implies a lower than healthy weight. My concern stems from my 10 years of private practice in our town of Branford as a certified eating disorder (ED) specialist. Many of my clients are referred to me from the Yale–New Haven Pediatric ED Unit, with significant weight

*loss, abnormal labs, and a diagnosis of anorexia nervosa or
bulimia nervosa. Most perceive themselves as fat and strive
to be skinny. This is a goal they seek at any expense. Yes, we
may live in a culture which teaches children that skinny is
more important than health. However, do we need to create
such a climate here in our Branford community? I ask that
we, as adults, be more mindful of the labels we use to identify
people. This is especially important in relation to food columns.
Please consider these facts: The symptoms of anorexia nervosa
(AN) are likely to include obsessive, intrusive thoughts and
food rituals. It is not uncommon for my clients to read recipes
to satisfy their hunger; in the past decade, ED hospitals have
increased by 119 percent for children under the age of 12;
and Connecticut now has a residential ED facility for 10- to
16-year-olds. For more information on eating disorders, go to
www.nationaleatingdisorders.org.*

Gina Macdonald MA, LPC, CEDS

Here are the results of a "professional to professional" strategic
letter.

*In 2007, after two young models succumbed to eating
disorders, Margo Maine, a founder of the National Eating
Disorders Association (NEDA), and Lynn Grefe, past CEO
of NEDA, jointly reached out to Diane Von Furstenberg, the
newly appointed President of the Council of Fashion Designers
in America, in the hopes of developing "a partnership or
collaborative relationship." The intent was to gain both a
deeper understanding of and respect for the fashion industry,
encouraging its potential leadership role to assist in "crucial
and transformative impact on women's health across the
globe"...meeting and discussing ways "to make the industry
safer for those it affects directly (models and student models)"
as well as all women. Despite Maine and Grefe's intention and
attempt, continued deaths occur (another model in 2010).
Through their persistent attempts the Council of Fashion
Designers in America implemented minor changes such as*

limiting the hours for models under 18 years of age to not
exceed midnight; the age of models to be 16 years or older;
supplying food for models at long photo shoots and providing
education about eating disorders. (Maine, 2017)

Another national level strategist, Sara Ziff, protects teenagers subject to pressure in a highly competitive business and industry that promotes thinness, allows poor working conditions, and overlooks sexual harassment. In 2012, Ziff, a former model turned activist founded the Model Alliance to give models a voice in their work. Six years later, executive director Ziff, along with models Coco Rocha and Milla Jovovich, reconstructed Model Alliance as a nonprofit research, policy, and advocacy organization in the fashion industry. Given a platform for their voice, many have come forth with allegations of misconduct, including sexual harassment.

It is important to note that changes come from everyday people using their voice as a strategy, stemming from an intention of good will. Health advocate Deepak Chopra says in *The Seven Spiritual Laws of Success* that "intention is the starting point of every dream." He adds, "The only caution is that you use your intent for the benefit of mankind" (1994, p. 72).

Experiential Task 16 TAKING CARE OF UNFINISHED BUSINESS

Psychodrama is a form of psychotherapy in which patients act out unresolved events from their past. The field was founded by Jacob L. Moreno. While studying in expressive arts therapy at Lesley College in the 1980s, I had the opportunity to add an elective, and I chose a class titled Psychodrama Techniques. Psychodramatist Peter Rowen, known as one of the pioneers of psychodrama who trained under Dr. Moreno, instructed us in this intense and dynamic form of therapy with a gentleness and compassion that reinforced the importance of client safety.

One exercise he mastered and which I find useful is called the Empty Chair. This technique originated in gestalt therapy under the direction of Fritz Pearls and has since then been incorporated into psychodrama therapy. I recommend it be practiced with a trained specialist—one with academic knowledge of drama therapy, psychodrama, or gestalt therapy—in a safe place where direct expression is encouraged on a bodily level.

Alexander Lowen, mentioned as a mind/body specialist, speaks of the "armoring" and "shielding" one builds after years of holding and/or repressing strong negative emotions (1993). Here we see how one's suppressed power, strength, and energy create a depression that may manifest as lethargy, exhaustion, fatigue, loss of appetite, or withdrawal from others. Enacting the body and mind to express strongly held emotions, as in the Empty Chair technique, allows for releasing those repressed emotions and opening up to a full range of feelings, as clients transition from simply verbalizing something toward a fuller experience using affect, cognition, and body.

> GUIDANCE: In working with others, do not begin with deep old wounds, but rather with a more recent life situation, nor is this method recommended for use with an emotionally upset or traumatized client. This precautionary measure allows more comfort with this method before proceeding to deeper therapeutic work.

TASK: The Empty Chair Technique

PROP: An empty chair

PREP: The client positions herself or himself in relation to the empty chair. Note: Facing the imagined person will empower the client. Clients are instructed to:

1. Invite the (imagined) person to sit in the empty chair.

2. Describe and introduce the person sitting in the chair.

3. Explain why the person was asked to come.

4. Directly tell the person how you feel toward him or her and what led you to feel that way, including how long you have felt that way.

5. Share how the past experience has affected your body image and your life, including any positive or negative ramifications.

6. Express any other related feelings you have in your life today.

7. Decide when/if you feel finished. Say goodbye.

★ *FOLLOW-UP GUIDANCE: Following the experience, clients return the group. Explore any feelings or strong emotions they experienced while in the role (e.g., control or lack of control, anger, etc.). Acknowledge and encourage feedback from peers to support the client's experience. (Adapted from Peter Rowen's teachings at Lesley College, 1982)*

ALLOWING FOR POSSIBILITY

Experiential Task 17 PRACTICING GRATITUDE

Your story unfolds as you experience changes; you learn of your "core of goodness" and practice self-care in response to this newfound knowledge. Realizing that there is a larger context through which to see your story and connect with all living beings will cultivate gratitude.

Gratitude is not a denial of life's problems and issues, nor does it come easy. Practice gratitude as you practice daily coping skills. Old styles of thinking may get in the way, insisting on making you a victim. Stay with your softer heart and keep your intention clear, stay in touch with your support system (whoever that should be), and reach out for professional help when needed.

Gratitude stones are pocket-size stones designed to be held while one expresses gratitude. The belief is that you are forming a new habit (if practiced daily) to feel grateful as opposed to feeling ungrateful for life. This stems from the theory that like attracts like. "The law of attraction will certainly and unerringly bring to you the conditions, environment and experiences in life, corresponding with your habitual, characteristic, predominant mental attitude" (Hannel, 1910).

PROP: A palm-size stone

1. Instruct your client to hold a stone and do the following:

2. Tonight, reflect on one moment from the day that you are thankful for.

3. Each and every night, around the same time, do the same, making it a habit to have a positive thought.

4. Each night following the above task, record your gratitude in a gratitude journal.

Experiential Task 18 FREE STYLE AND
IMPROVISATIONAL DANCE/MOVEMENT

The ADTA refers to dance/movement therapy (DMT) as "the psychotherapeutic use of movement, a process that furthers emotional, cognitive, social and physical integration of the individual" (2016). Dance/movement therapists use this psychotherapeutic modality as a vehicle for expression of a more genuine or "authentic self" by guiding clients to reconnect with their body and emotions. While engaging in body image disturbance symptomology (excessive worry regarding weight, body surveillance, and objectification of body, bingeing, restriction or purging), clients are not connected to their bodily sensations, nor are they connecting their emotions to a felt body sense. Dance/movement therapist Susan Kleinman speaks to this disconnection and its aftermath: "Ignoring internal states amounts to burying feelings, and the burial site exists in that body itself" (Kleinman & Hall, 2006). This visually strong statement paints the important work for therapists to address as they attempt to dismantle body image disturbance, making it is possible for clients to gradually reinhabit their bodies.

While body image therapy and movement-therapy sessions invite clients to engage on a body level, their fear, resistance, and boundary disturbance are understandable, in that they have not connected with their bodies for some time. Expecting them to stand up and participate in a task is unreasonable, as they may not know how to connect directly into their body. Their tendency to avoid feelings and sensations has led them to a "standoff," with their body and head in conflict. Safety in a group is more challenging and necessary. Here we see the "pre-affiliation stage" of I. D. Yalom's group development theory applicable in one's need to feel comfortable with others. Safety provided through the therapist's structure will allow them to "approach and avoid" at their own discretion. In time, they advance to find affiliations by discovering a commonality with the others. Yalom's next "stage of Power and Control" shows individuals struggling for their autonomy through risk-taking and new communicative behaviors. This stage is necessary for group cohesiveness as members look to safety before sharing their personal stories. It is here that clients move from resistance and "awkwardness" into more personal involvement (Yalom, 1970). Developmental stages continue reaching intimacy until a group ends or terminates. However, with new clients entering the group sessions each week, there is a need to shift back to developing affiliations and rebuilding trust—assisting newcomers to invest in the group as a healing place. As a group therapist, I have been reminded via client feedback to provide verbal explanation of my task's theoretical background and purpose prior to asking for involvement. This will increase the comfort level and participation in each stage of group development.

All stages of group development can be experienced through movement, which creates and expresses meaning, just as words do. When moving physically with others as in dance/movement therapy sessions, participants can explore nonverbal expressions as valid forms of communication between members, encouraging trust and closeness while building a physical and emotional safety zone. Here we have a chance to develop a special connection with the client through an acquired therapeutic skill called kinesthetic empathy. "Kinesthetic empathy is the ability, on a bodily level, to understand what others are feeling" (Kleinman, 2013). This level of connecting via movement exploration between client and therapist provides the client validation on a bodily level, which is crucial to enhancing body image. Whether it be full body movement or simply a changing facial expression, when the authenticity emerges and is validated by another, a human developmental process is reset; a way of reassembling (integration and conceptualizing) one's senses into a more cohesive body image, similar to what occurs through childhood in developmental learning. This growing awareness of self, and trust of the body as self, continue through exploring and navigating one's psychosocial world.

TASK: Exploring movement qualities. This serves as a warm-up exercise for participants, both physically and emotionally.

"Movement quality" is considered "an aspect of behavior," according to Rudolf Laban, a dancer and choreographer who founded a "method of describing changes in movement quality" called Effort/Shape. The Dance Notation Bureau's handbook *Primer for Movement Description* contains his original formulations (Dell, 1970, pp. 7, 11–12). These guidelines assist dance/movement therapists working with child development, rehabilitation, and psychological research, as well as professional dancers and actors. Flow, weight, time, and space are called "effort factors," each with a range between two opposite extremes of a movement vocabulary. Clinically, this method of exploring and expanding our movement repertoire helps clients connect to their body to trust their creative impulses, while learning from interacting with others.

PROPS: Music of your choice and space to move freely in

GUIDANCE: Allow 2–4 minutes with each directive

1. Stand and move with the rhythm of the music.

2. Find and explore "FLOW" movement qualities (bound flow and free flow). Bound flow is like wringing out a face cloth, and free flow is movement as in slashing or brushing. Is there a middle or even place?

3. Move with different qualities of "TIME" (sustained or sudden) as you choose. Can you try slow motion? Is fast familiar to you? Try both.

4. Feel the "SPACE" (direct and focused or indirect, as in multifocused) as you move through it. Can you focus directly on an object as you move toward it? Now try searching around for something lost, never quite finding it. Notice differing feelings and emotions that arise with each.

5. The final "effort factor" is "WEIGHT" ("light and strong") is explored. Use an image to help find the quality (e.g., "light and breezy clouds vs. heavy bag of groceries.") Note: "Center of weight refers to the part of the body most involved in initiating shifts of weight and generally activating and supporting body weight" (Dell, 1970, p. 22). The use of our center of weight helps us with producing light or strong qualities of movement.

6. Find your preferences by intertwining these to make a style all your own from your expanded movement vocabulary.

7. Continue until music ends and come back to your comfortable space in the room.

8. Discussing the experience, give each person a chance to describe what it felt like to move, acknowledging any feelings, preferences, or moments of awareness of self or others.

TASK: Freestyle/improvisation

Dance improvisation is more of a spontaneous style of movement than the guided style above. It requires letting go of preconceived ideas and allowing intuition to carry you into new movement qualities, shapes, dimensions, levels—without conscious intention. This is the practice of self-trust on a bodily level, a way to trust your body, to give permission to act in a more uninhibited manner—not to be censoring or monitoring your body. A very different way to be "in charge"—learning to rely on self—this serves as a metaphor for recovery as clients trust their instincts, feelings, and confidence in their ability to be in charge of their life (Kleinman, 2013).

1. Standing in circle, facing each other, connect with the rhythm of the music.

2. The leader displays a gesture and all are invited to try it together (repeat 4–5 times, paying attention to the quality of the movement).

3. The person to the right adapts a new gesture and quality from the original gesture. Let it begin from the previous movement—not your head or a preconceived idea (repeat 4–5 times).

4. The next person begins where the last left off, morphing into another gesture (repeat 4–5 times).

5. Continue around the room, giving each participant a chance to express directly from the body in a spontaneous manner—trusting on a bodily level.

6. Return to the leader, who finds a uniting gesture or phrase to end (repeat 4–5 times).

7. Pause and discuss the experience. Ask: what movement do you prefer and why? what feelings did you notice when moving?

Experiential Task 19 EXPRESSIVE/RECEPTIVE MOVEMENT

This task is to mobilize, release, and replenish your emotional wellspring.

PROP: A medium-size pillow

PREP: Clients stand in a circle formation

> GUIDANCE: Spend 3–5 minutes on each step before moving onto the next step.

TASK: Pillow Throwing

Ask clients to:

1. Throw the pillow to each other back and forth, cross parallel, catching and throwing quickly. (mobilize energy)

2. Name a color while you throw the pillow quickly to each other—"fuchsia," "teal," "yellow." (encourage spontaneity)

3. Name a feeling while you throw the pillow to another— "love," "sadness," "joy." (help identify feelings)

4. Next, let go of one feeling or emotion you do not want in your life as you throw the pillow onto the floor—"shame." (encourage connecting and emotional expression)

5. Take back a feeling or emotion as you receive the pillow from another. For example: "I want self-trust." (teach receptivity)

Simple as this task sounds, if explored deeply it can be intense, as participants lessen self-censoring and engage spontaneously while choosing what to "release" and what to "reclaim" in the process of recovery. Often a client will feel hopeless and not conceive of anything to "receive" or "take back." Here therapists can model for the client, drawing on examples from previous sessions. E.g., "Someone once said they wanted to take back self-dignity." Depending on the strength of the group, the therapist's role changes from one of acknowledgment to one of encouragement.

I am reminded of how creatively the process unfolds, as the group will create a dynamic place to "throw away" painful emotions—one after another after another—inspiring each other to release their pain. "Go ahead, throw away feeling self-conscious, you don't need that." The task includes an opportunity to "take back" positive feelings, planting seeds for growth. "I take back hope." "I take back life." Providing them with group structure, they will facilitate a unique creative process, transitioning from "holding it in" to "throwing it away." Similarly, they shift from "being in control" to "letting go of control"—"yielding to their authentic impulses"—to create a natural flow of energy from within. (Kleinman, 2013).

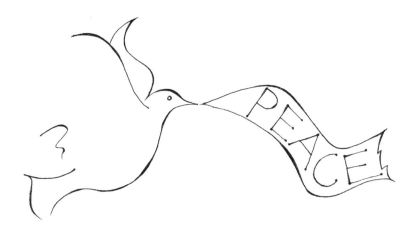

Experiential Task 20 FIVE SIMPLE MINDFUL
TECHNIQUES FOR LIFTING THE BODY IMAGE BLUES

These mini self-help steps can lift you up out of a bad body image day.
The more you use them, the more natural they will become.

TASK: Practicing Mindful Body Image

1. When you feel particularly down on yourself or your body,
   ask yourself if you are distorting your body image and do a
   simple body image inquiry. Take a grounding breath, close
   your eyes, and see yourself in your mind's eye. Now, reach
   your real arms to where you believe your body part (say
   waist) is. Pause, take a complete breath cycle (in-breath
   into out-breath). Now, open your eyes to note the difference
   between where your hands are and where your waist actually
   is. Stay full of noticing and empty of judgment.

2. Practice keeping this knowledge with you to remind you that
   you might carry a perception of yourself that differs from
   how others see you. If your negative feeling returns, just
   notice how you respond to the feeling. This may be charged
   and/or negative. Breathe another complete breath cycle
   and ask yourself, "Could I allow for the possibility that my
   subjective image differs from objective fact?" Yes, it takes

years to change a perceptual distortion and yes, we can change how we respond to it—right here, right now!

3. We all have a sense of what we want to look like. Notice if your ideal image allows for your unique physical traits. Have you abandoned your body's positive traits? Could you incorporate a positive trait of yourself into your ideal image? To build from a place of self is to be authentic. If it is too difficult to find a positive trait; ask someone you trust to help you. She or he may find a positive trait that you cannot. Could you allow for their perception to be true? If this is difficult, acknowledge how powerful your feelings and perceptions are.

4. Body image and self-esteem are interconnected. Is it possible to rely on self-esteem to support a poor body image? Ask yourself this question: "Do I need to hold negative ideas and feelings that deny me a chance to enjoy being?" If so, keep in mind that every person who has gained compassion toward himself or herself has also experienced self-hatred for one reason or another. This is part of being human, as it teaches us humility.

5. If you have come this far, you are a warrior! You are willing to go to places that are uncomfortable to you. Stay grounded. Talk to your therapist or a trusted friend about your experience and your practice of these steps. The shift from distortion to clarity will take time, but eventually you will see more clearly and discover "the essence of your being" or "the core of (your) goodness" (Schiffmann, 1996, pp. 13–15). Discovering this can be an exciting opportunity to design, choreograph, and identify who you are in this world—even with the challenges and setbacks that come unexpectedly and unfairly in life.

GLOSSARY

Sources: NEDA, HOPE, Dictionary of Psychology,
The Oxford Dictionary, and Wikipedia

American Art Therapy Association (AATA): Founded in 1969 an educational organization dedicated to the growth and development of the art therapy profession. www.aata.org.

American Dance/Movement Therapy Association (ADTA): Founded in 1966 to establish and maintain standards of professional education in the field of dance/movement therapy (www.adta.org).

American Drama Therapy Association (NADTA): Incorporated in 1979 to establish and uphold standards of professional competence and ethics among drama therapists and promote the profession of drama therapy through information and advocacy (www.nadta.org).

Anorexia nervosa (AN): An eating disorder defined by weight loss and severely low weight relative to stature, distorted perception of body, illogical fear of weight gain, and amenorrhea (loss of menstruation).

Binge eating disorder (BED): An eating disorder characterized by recurrent episodes of eating large quantities of food with feelings of loss of control followed by shame or guilt.

Body awareness: One's ability to understand where their body is in space, how they move—a sense that one has of their own body.

Body concept: The evaluative representation of one's own body, with special emphasis on how it appears to others.

Body image (BI): A mental representation of oneself whether in motion or stillness derived from sensations, contact, emotional experiences, and postural changes. Known also as a psychological experience that focuses on perceptions and attitudes toward one's body.

Body image dissatisfaction: When one experiences extreme dislike for his or her body, either as a whole or regarding specific body parts.

Body image distortion: When one believes his or her weight, body parts, or size differs significantly from what people see.

Body image disturbance: An internalizing of a thin ideal image, body dissatisfaction, and distorted perceptions of one's body image.

Body image therapy: This form of therapy addresses the body directly to create a more healthful body image using movement, interaction, and awareness.

Body Dismorphic Disorder (BDD): A preoccupation with minimal or nonexistent flaws in appearance.

Body esteem: The level or degree of positiveness and importance one attributes to their body and body appearance.

Body schema: An overall pattern of one's sensory awareness, a pattern of coenesthesia (impressions arising from sensations).

Body shaming: The practice of humiliating someone by making critical comments about body or size.

Body stalking: Comments made about others body types, spoken or via social networking.

Body protest: Physical symptoms that express a protest against the circumstances one is placed in.

Boundaries: A line that marks the beginning of an area—a dividing line. Personal boundaries are the physical, emotional, and mental limits we establish.

Boundary disturbance: Refers to a degree of avoidance and contact. Anorexics show greater disturbance or anxiety surrounding connections, exposure, and emotional closeness. This can be reflective of a breakdown in self-other boundaries.

Bulimia nervosa (BN): An eating disorder marked by bingeing and followed by self-induced vomiting or other compensatory behaviors.

Center: An intangible place inside oneself which serves as the place of the inner voice and source of one's inner guidance.

Compartmentalizing: A defense mechanism or coping strategy to avoid mental discomfort. To separate into isolated parts as in focusing on specific body parts.

Eating disorder (ED): A range of psychological disorders characterized by abnormal or disturbed eating habits.

Emotional disconnect: A conscious unawareness of the body due to overregulated emotions leaving one without connection to his/her emotional state. Sometimes referred to as "body disconnect."

Experiential Therapy: Techniques using expressive skills such as role play, guided imagery, art or movement to re-experience emotions under the guidance of a trained experiential therapist.

Kinesthesia: One's perception of body position and movement of muscles, joints, and tendons.

Kinesthetic awareness: One's ability to experience feelings and sensations inwardly, based on proprioception (sense of relative position of neighboring parts of the body).

Kinesthetic empathy: One's ability to experience empathy by observing the movements of another person.

Maladaptive coping strategies: Strategies for coping that increase stress rather than decrease stress.

Meditation: A practice whereby one trains the mind or induces a mode of consciousness. Also refers to a broad variety of practices designed to promote relaxation and to develop compassion, patience, generosity, and forgiveness.

Perceptual distortions: Incorrect understandings or abnormal interpretations of a perceptual experience.

Proprioceptive: Relating to the stimuli connected to movement, position, and balance within an organism.

Self-concept: The idea of the self based on beliefs one holds true about oneself, and responses from others.

Self-esteem: A measure of how much one feels they are worth and how they are valued, as in confidence or self-respect.

Self-image: The self one thinks oneself to be; includes character, status, body, and body appearance.

Self-reflection: Meditation or serious thought about one's character, actions, and motives.

Social media: Computer-based technologies that facilitate the creation and sharing of information, ideas, and personal information. Can be a way for youth to learn what is acceptable as well as how to interact with peers.

Subpersonalities: Pieces of the whole of the overall personality, which have a life of their own.

Triggers: An event or circumstance that produces uncomfortable symptoms. The cause of every trigger is inside—meaning inner work can heal it.

REFERENCES

Alexander, D. (2001). "Bullying Widespread in U.S. Schools, Survey Finds" http://www.nichd.nih.gov. Retrieved on 1/25/2017.

American Dance Therapy Association (ADTA) (2016). "What is Dance/Movement Therapy?" https://adta.org/Default.aspx?pageld. Retrieved on 10/30/2017.

American Psychiatric Association (1987). *Diagnostic and Statistical Manual of Mental Disorders* (3rd ed.). Washington, DC: American Psychiatric Association.

Anderson, D. A., Lavender, J. M., & De Young, K. P. (2010). "The Assessment Process: Redefining the Clinical Evaluation of Patients with Eating Disorders." In M. Maine, B. Hartman McGilley, & D. W. Bunnell (Eds.), *Treatment of Eating Disorders: Bridging the Research-Practice Gap* (pp. 72–73, 81). New York, NY: Academic.

Barry, A. J. (2016, November). "Words Matter in Matters of Gender Equality and Role Modeling." *Branford Sound,* Home/Living Section (pp. 3, 10). https://www.zip06.com.

Benson, H., & Klipper, M. Z. (1976). *The Relaxation Response.* New York, NY: Harper Torch.

Bloomfield H., Colgrove, M., & McWilliams, P. (1976, 1991). *How to Survive the Loss of a Love* (p. 3). Los Angeles, CA: Prelude.

BBC News (2005, March 7). "Six-Year-Olds 'Want to be Thin.' " http:// news.bbc.co.uk/go/pr/fr/-/2/hi/health/4319105.stm. Retrieved on 3/7/2005.

Boris, H. N. (1984). "The Problem of Anorexia Nervosa." *International Journal of Psychoanalysis, 66,* 315–322.

Borysenko, J. Z. (1988*). Minding the Body, Mending the Mind* (p. 212). Reading, MA: Addison-Wesley.

Bunnell, D. W. (2011). "A Word from the Editor." *Perspectives* (p. 1). Retrieved from http://renfrewcenter.com/sites/default/ files/2011%20winter%20perspectives%202.4.150.pdf.

Canner, N. (1968). *...And a Time to Dance.* Boston, MA: Beacon.

Cash, T. F. (2004). "Cognitive Behavioral Perspectives on Body Image." In T. F. Cash & T. Pruzinsky (Eds.), *Body Image: A Handbook of Theory, Research and Clinical Practice* (p. 43). New York, NY: Guilford.

Cash, T. F. (2004). "Beyond Traits: Assessing Body Image States." In T. F. Cash & T. Pruzinsky (Eds.), *Body Image: A Handbook of Theory, Research and Clinical Practice* (p. 163). New York, NY: Guilford.

Cash, T. F., & Pruzinsky, T. (2004). "Assessing Body Image and Quality of Life in Medical Settings." In T. Cash & T. Pruzinsky (Eds.), *Body Image: A Handbook of Theory, Research and Clinical Practice* (pp. 170–177). New York, NY: Guilford.

Cash, T. F. (2008). *The Body Image Workbook*: *An Eight-Step Program for Learning to Like Your Looks* (2nd ed., p. 112). Oakland, CA: New Harbinger.

Cash, T. F. (2012). *The Encyclopedia of Body Image and Human Development.* New York, NY: Academic.

Chopra, D. (1994). *The Seven Spiritual Laws of Success: A Practical Guide to the Fulfillment of Your Dreams* (p. 65). San Rafael, CA: Amber-Allen Publishing and New World Library.

Cloak, N. (2011). "Psychodynamic Therapy and Symptom Management: A New Dialectic of Understanding and Action." *Perspectives* (pp. 13–16). Retrieved from http://renfrewcenter.com/sites/default/files/2011%20winter%20perspectives%202.4.150.pdf.

Cohn, P. (2016). *"Can Sports Improve Young Athletes' Self-Esteem?" Retrieved 3/17/2017 from http://www.youthsportspsychology.com.*

Cope, S. (2000). *Yoga and the Quest for the True Self.* New York, N Y: Bantam.

Crosky, C., & Huston, L. (1994). *What Does a Healthy Body Image Look Like? Eating Disorder View.* Publication of Brattleboro Retreat.

Dalichow, I. (1996). *Aura-Soma: Healing Through Color, Plant and Crystals Energy* (pp. 217–225). Carlsbad, CA: Hay House.

Daignault, E., Macdonald, M., & Yang, J. (2012, March 21). "Westport Youth Group Launches a Kindness Project." Retrieved from www.westportdailyvoice.com.

Daubenmier, J. (2005). "The Relationship of Yoga, Body Awareness and Body Responsiveness to Self-Objectification and Disordered Eating." *Psychology of Women Quarterly, 29* (2)207–219.

Dell, C. (1970). *A Primer for Movement Description: Using Effort/Shape and Supplementary Concepts* (pp. 5–7, 12–13). New York, NY: Dance Notation Bureau.

De Waal, F. (2017). *The Age of Empathy: Nature's Lessons for a Kinder Society.* New York, NY: Three Rivers.

Dokter, D. (1995). *Arts Therapies and Clients with Eating Disorders: Fragile Board* (p. 3). London: Jessica Kingsley.

Erikson, E. H. (1950). *Childhood and Society: The Landmark Work on Social Significance of Childhood* (pp. 247–274). New York, NY: W. W. Norton.

Fisher, S. (1990). "The Evolution of Psychological Concepts About the Body." In T. F. Cash & T. Pruzinsky (Eds.), *Body Images: Development, Deviance, and Change* (pp. 3–20). New York, NY: Guilford.

Fisher, S., & Cleveland, S. (1968). *Body Image and Personality* (2nd rev. ed.).New York, NY: Dover.

Franzoi, S. L., & Shields, S. (1984, April). "The Body Image Scale: Multidimensional Structure and Sex Differences in a College Population." *Journal of Personality Assessment, 4* (2), 173–178.

Girl Scout Study (2010). "Who's That Girl? Image and Social Media Survey." Retrieved on 4/10/18 from https://www.girlscout.org/research.

Hannel, C. F. (1910). *The Master Key System*. Rockville, MD: Manor Thrift.

Hutchinson, M. G. (1985). *Transforming Body Image: Learning to Love the Body You Have* (pp. 116, 123, 216). Freedom, CA: Crossing.

Johnston, A. (2010). "Body Talk: The Use of Metaphor and Storytelling in Body Image Treatment." In M. Maine, B. Hartman McGilley, & D. W. Bunnell (Eds.), *Treatment of Eating Disorders: Bridging the Research-Practice Gap* (p. 445). New York, NY: Academic.

Kabat-Zinn, J. (1990). "The Foundations of Mindfulness Practice: Attitudes and Commitment." In J. Kabat-Zinn (Ed.), *Full Catastrophic Living: Using the Wisdom of Your Body and Mind to Face Stress, Pain and Illness* (pp. 31–40). New York, NY: Random House.

Klein, M., & Guest-Kelly, A. (2010*). Yoga and Body Image: 25 Personal Stories about Beauty, Bravery and Loving Your Body*. Woodbury, MN: Llewellyn.

Kleinman, S. (2013). "Dance/Movement Therapy Can Connect Mind and Body." Retrieved on 9/25/17 from: https://www.eatingdisorderhope.com/treatment-for-eating-disorders/types-of-treatment/body-movement-dance-therapy/professional-techniques.

Kleinman, S. (2015). "Becoming Whole Again: Dance Movement Therapy for Individuals with Eating Disorders." In S. Chaiklin & H. Wengrower (Eds.), *The Art and Science of Dance/Movement Therapy: Life is Dance* (2nd ed., pp. 139–158). New York, NY: Routledge.

Kleinman, S., & Hall, T. (2006). "Dance/Movement Therapy: A Method for Embodying Emotions." In W. Davis & S. (Eds.), *Healing Through Relationships Series: Contributions to Eating Disorder Theory and Treatment,* vol. 1: *Fostering Body-Mind Integration.* Philadelphia: Renfew Center Foundation.

Koffka, Kurt. (2016). "Gestalt Psychology." Wikipedia. Retrieved on 3/06/2017 from http://www.en.m.wikipedia.org.

Kolata, G. (2016, May 2). "After 'The Biggest Loser,' Their Bodies Fought Back to Regain Weight." *New York Times.* Retrieved on 4/04/2017 from https://mobile.nytimes.com.

Krueger, D. W. (2002). "Psychodynamic Perspectives on Body Image: Stages in the Development of Body Image." In T.F. Cash & T. Pruzinsky (Eds.), *Body Image: A Handbook for Theory, Research and Clinical Practice* (pp. 32–33). New York, NY: Guilford.

Lenehan, M. M. (1997). "Validation and Psychotherapy." In A. Bohart & L. Greenberg (Eds.), *Empathy Reconsidered: New Directions* in Psychotherapy (pp. 353–391). Washington, DC: APA.

Lenhart A., Purcell, K., Smith, A., & Zickuhr, K. (2010). "Social Media and Young Adults." (Part 3: Social Media.) Retrieved on 4/5/2018 from http://www.pewinternet.org/2010/02/03/part-3-social-media.

Lougren, S. (2005, Aug.). "Chimps, Humans 96 Percent the Same, Gene Study Finds." Retrieved February 2017 from https://news.nationalgeographic.com/news/2005/08/0831_chimp_genes.html.

Lowen, A. D. (1993). *Depression and the Body: The Biological Basis of Faith and Reality.* Ontario: Penguin.

Ludwig, D. (2016). "Dr. David Ludwig Explains the Biggest Loser Syndrome." Retrieved on 5/12/2017 from https://www.news wgbh.org.

Maine, M. (2017). Personal Communication.

Maine, M. (2000). *Body Wars: Making Peace with Women's Bodies. An Activist's Guide* (pp. 83, 100–101). Carlsbad, CA: Gurze.

Maine, M., & Bunnell, D.W. (2010). "A Perfect Biopsychosocial Storm: Gender, Culture, and Eating Disorders." In M. Maine, B. H. McGilley & D. W. Bunnell (Eds)., *Treatment of Eating Disorders: Bridging the Research-Practice Gap* (pp. 3–4). New York, NY: Academic.

Maine, M., & Kelly, J. (2005). *The Body Myth: Adult Women and the Pressure to be Perfect* (p. 183). Hoboken, NJ: Wiley.

MEDA (1999). Multi-Service Eating Disorder Association (formerly Massachusetts Eating Disorder Association). https://www.medainc.org.

Maslin, S. (2016, Sept. 29). "Trump Comments Fuel Dialogue on Fat-Shaming." *New York Times*. http://www.nytimes.com.

Myers, L. (2013). "The Power of the Spoken Word: 'The Shrinking Women.' " Retrieved on 8/8/2017 from https://sites.psu.edu/passionoboudiyat/2017/02/10/lily-myers-shrinking-women.

Nardozzi, J. (2009). Renfrew Connections: Physical Hunger vs. Emotional Hunger (pp. 1–3).

NEDA (2010). "Factors That May Contribute to Eating Disorders." www.nationaleatingdisorders.org.

NEDIA National Eating Disorders Information Center. www.nedic.ca.

Neumark-Sztainer, D. (2005). *"I'm, Like, SO Fat!" Helping Your Teen Make Healthy Choices about Eating and Exercise in a Weight-Obsessed World* (pp. 46, 62–63). New York, NY: Guilford.

Neumark-Sztainer, D., Wall, M., Guo, J., Story, M., Haines, J., & Eisenberg, M. (2006). "Obesity, Disordered Eating and Eating Disorders in a Longitudinal Study of Adolescents: How Do Dieters Fare Five Years Later?" *Journal of the American Dietetic Association, 106,* 559–568.

Nin, A. (1969). *The Diary of Anaïs Nin. Volume 1, 1931–1934.* (New York, NY: Harcourt).

PBS (2017). *Spy in the Wild.* www.pbs.org/nature/spy-wild-nature-mini-series. Viewed Feb. 1, 2017.

Peck, T. (2016) New York City Dance Project. In: K.Browas and D. Ory (Eds.) *The Art of Movement.* New York, NY: Black Dog & Leventhal.

Perls, F. (2013). *Gestalt Therapy Verbatim.* Gouldsboro, ME: Gestalt Journal Press.

Pew Research (2005). Prader-Willi Research Foundation. www.pewresearch.org.

Pollock, J. P. (1949, Aug. 8). "The Art Story." Retrieved from *Life* on 5/12/2017. https://www.theartstory.org.

Project EAT II. (2004). "Eating and Attitudes in Teens." Retrieved on 4/5/17 from http://www.sphresearch.umn.edu/epi/project-eat/#EAT2.

Psychology Today Online. "Soft Chalk." Retrieved on 2/11/2018 from https://www.softchalk.com.

Renfrew Center Foundation. (2010). *Understanding Body Image Problems.* "Signs of Body Image Disturbance". (p. 3).

Ressler, A., Kleinman, S. A., & Mott E. (2010). *The Use of Holistic Methods to Integrate the Shattered Self.* In M. Maine, B. Hartman McGilley, & D. W. Bunnell (Eds.), *Treatment of Eating Disorders: Bridging the Research-Practice Gap* (pp. 406, 413). New York, NY: Academic.

Ressler, A., & Kleinman, S. (2012). *Experiential and Somatopsychic Approaches to Body Image Change.* Thomas F. Cash (Ed.), *Encyclopedia of Body Image and Human Appearance,* vol. 1, pp. 418–424. San Diego, CA: Academic.

Rico, G. (2000). *Writing the Natural Way: Using Right-Brain Techniques to Release Your Expressive Powers* (2nd rev. ed., pp. 16–23). New York, NY: Tarcher Putnam.

Roberts, T. A. (2004, May/June). Positive i.d. (p. 108). *Yoga Journal.*

Ruskey-Rabinor, J., & Bilich, M. (2004). "Experiential Approaches to Changing Body Image." In T. Cash & T. Pruzinsky (Eds)., *Body Image: A Handbook of Theory, Research and Clinical Practice* (pp. 469–475). New York, NY: Guilford.

Ryan, R. S., & Travis, J. (1991). *Wellness: Small Changes You Can Use to Make a Big Difference.* Berkeley, CA: Ten Speed.

Sebastian, M. (2017, June). "Thirty Times Donald Trump Has Been Completely Insulting to Women." Retrieved on 6/30/2017 from http://www.cosmopolitan.com.

Sell, C. (2003). *Yoga from the Inside Out: Making Peace with Your Body Through Yoga.* (pp.51-53). Prescott, AZ: Hohm.

Schiffmann, E. (1996). *Yoga: The Spirit and Practice of Moving into Stillness* (pp. 3, 4, 7, 11–13, 15, 23, 45, 57, 309). New York, NY: Simon and Schuster.

Schwartz, R. C. (2001). *Introduction to the Internal Family Systems Model* (pp. 44, 89–90, 103–104, 115–116, 144). Oak Park, IL: Trailheads.

Sesan, R. (2009). "Forgiveness: The Final Frontier in Recovery from an Eating Disorder." In M. Maine, W. N. Davis, & J. Shure (Eds.), *Effective Clinical Practice in the Treatment of Eating Disorders: The Heart of the Matter* (pp. 235, 244). New York, NY: Routledge.

Smith, E. R., & Mackie, D. M. (2007). Self-Esteem. Wikipedia. https://en.mwikipedia.org.

Smith-Theodore, D. (2015). *TuTu Thin: A Guide to Dancing Without an Eating Disorder* (p. 85). Calabasas, CA: Tu Tu Publications.

Stepanek, M. J. T. (2002). *Journey Through Heartsongs* (p. 49). Alexandria, Va.: VSP Books. www.MattieOnline.com. "Swinging" used with permission from publisher.

The Model Alliance: A New Model for Fashion.(2017). www.modelalliance.org.

Totenbier, S. L. (1995). "A New Way of Working with Body Image in Therapy, Incorporating Dance/Movement Therapy Methodology." In D. Dokter (Ed.), *Arts Therapies and Clients with Eating Disorders: Fragile Board* (pp. 193, 195). London: Jessica Kingsley.

Turlington, C. (2002). *Living Yoga: Creating a Life Practice* (p. 95). New York, NY: Hyperion.

Waxman, S. G. "Higher Cortical Functions." Chapter 21 (2016) In S. G. Waxman (Ed.), *Clinical Neuroanatomy,* 27th ed. New York, NY: McGraw-Hill Education. Retrieved on 4/27/16 from https://accessmedicine.mhmedical.com.

Willliamson, D. A., Stewart, T. M., White, M. A., & York-Crowe, E. (2004). "An Information-Processing Perspective on Body Image." In T. Cash and T. Pruzinsky (Eds.), *Body Image: A Handbook of Theory, Research and Clinical Practice* (p. 53). New York, NY: Guilford.

Yalom, I. D. (1970). *The Theory and Practice of Group Psychotherapy* (pp. 231–244). New York, NY: HarperCollins.

Young, M. (1995). "Dramatherapy in Short-Term Groupwork with Women with Bulimia." In D. Dokter (Ed.), *Arts Therapies and Clients with Eating Disorders: Fragile Board* (p. 111). London: Jessica Kingsley.

Zembrowski, J., Sussman, H., and McMillan, J. (2014). *The Upstander Movement: Teenage Guide to Being an Upstander.* Retrieved from https://newhavenacademy.files.wordpress.com/2015/12/handbook-2015-16.pdf.

Zinn, H. (2002). *You Can't Be Neutral on a Moving Train: A Personal History of Our Times* (p. 208). Boston, MA: Beacon.

ENDNOTES

"It's a complex world. Sometimes I feel like a chimpanzee." Hansen, D.(1977). *It's a Complex World*. Retrieved from http://www.genius. com/DavidHansen-its-a-complex-world-lyrics..

"Don't try to understand it. Let it try and understand you. E.E. Cummings, *Tulips and Chimneys*. New York, NY: Liverright.

"I get this eerie feeling, So familiar to me now, It finds its way beneath my skin, And it lingers there somehow." Harrington, H.R.(2015) *I Don't Live Here Anymore*. Retrieved from http://www.ransompier. com/Hayley-Rose-Harrington-i-don't-live-here-anymore-lyrics.

"From out of the many particulars comes oneness and out of the oneness comes the many particulars." Heraclitus of Ephesus, https://www.picturequotes.com>heraclitus>oneness.

"Don't touch me I'm a real live wire." Byrnes, D. (1977). *Psycho Killer*. Retrieved from http://www.genius.com/David-Byrnes-psycho-killer-lyrics.

"I stand in awe of my body." Thoreau, H.D, Emerson, R.W.& Franklin, B.S. (1899). *The Writings of Henry David Thoreau*. Volume 3. (p. 95). New York, NY: Houghton Mifflin & Co.

"You have a paintbrush which can be used to transfer your insides onto the canvas of your life." Glennon Doyle Melton "Your body is not your masterpiece." *Huffington Post.* (August 5, 2014) https://www.huffingtonpost.com/glennon-melton/your-body-is-not-your-masterpiece_b_5586341.html.

"In the depth of winter, I finally learned that within me there lay an invincible summer." Camus, A. (2016). *Albert Camus Quotes.* Scottville, CA: Create Space Independent Publishing Platform.

"Change is the end result of true learning." Buscaglia, L. (1984). Loving Each Other. *The Challenge of Human Relationships.* New York, NY: Faucet Books Random House.

"Sometimes there is no next time - no time outs, no second chances. Sometimes it's just now or never." Alan Bennet, English playwright, screen actor, author (1934-present). www.goodreads>373053-sometimes-there-is-no-time-outs.

"There is no separation, only in the mind." Native American saying.

"When the well is dry, we know the worth of water." Franklin, B. (2016). *Benjamin Franklin's Virtues Journal.* A companion to *Benjamin Franklin's Book of Virtues.* Carlisre, MA: Applewood Book. Ingram Publisher Services.

"You know life fractures us into little pieces. It harms us but it's how we glue those fractures back together that make us stronger." Jones, Carrie (2010) *Entice* (Need#3) USA: Bloombury.

"To do is to be." Sarte, J.P.C.A (2017). Retrieved from: https.//www.google.com/amp/s/yourstory.com/2017/06/jean-paul-sarte-philosophy-existentialism-freedom/amp.

"To be is to be." Friedrich Nietzsche. Allen, E.L. (1986). *From Plato To Nietzsche.* A Fawcett Premier book. New York, NY: Random House .

"To be or not to be." Shakespeare, W. (1998). *A Book of Quotations.* Mineola, York, NY: Dover Publications.

"Yabba Dabba Doo." Reed, A. and Ohmart, B. (2013). *Yabba Dabba Doo! The Alan Reed Story*. Ashland, OR: Blackstone Audio Publishing.

"Do Be A Do Be." Claster, N. and Cladster, B. (1960). *The Romper Room of Do Be Manners*. New York, NY: Wonderbook.

"What will be will be." Day, D. (2006) *Que Sera, Sera: The Magic of Doris Day*. Albany, GA: Bear Manor Media.

"Just say what you want to say...and say it with all your heart." Gilbert, E. (2016). *Big Magic: Creative Living without Fear* (p. 98) New York, NY: Riverhead Books.

"It is only with the heart that one can see rightly. What is essential is invisible to the eye." Antoine de Saint-Exupery, *The Little Prince* (1943). USA: Reynal & Hitchcock.

"With your head full of brains and your shoes full of feet, Your too smart to go down any not so good street." Suess Geisel, T.(1990). *Oh! The Places You'll Go!* (p. 50) New York, NY: Random House.

"We do not see things as they are, we see them as we are." Nin, A.A.J.A.R.E.(1961) *The Seduction of the Minotaur*. Athens, Ohio: Swallow Press.

"Close your eyes and picture the sun." Pomponius Atticus. Source: www.quotecatalog.com.

GINA MACDONALD MA,LPC,CEDS. is a Licensed Professional Counselor working with the eating disorder population for over 25 years. Graduate degree training in the field of dance/movement therapy led to the area of body image. A Certified International Eating Disorder Specialist/Supervisor, Gina speaks passionately on college and university campuses to staff and students. Her work in ED treatment centers includes Hartford Hospital's Institute of Living, The Renfrew Center of CT, and with Walden Behavioral Care on the shoreline of Connecticut where she has held a Private Practice for 10 years.

CPSIA information can be obtained
at www.ICGtesting.com
Printed in the USA
FSHW021626081218

9 780692 188798